MW00638594

Here Comes the Sun

"In Lowitz's quest for harmony and beauty—the story of a mother, told by a poet through the self-examination of a yogi—she discovers that where there is fear there can be no love, and where there is a victim there can be no enlightenment. I fell in love with everyone in this memoir of a woman wanting to be loved and to love. This is an intimate, brilliant, beautiful offering."
—SHARON GANNON, Jivamukti Yoga

"We think we know where babies come from, but do we know how a mother is born? *Here Comes the Sun* is a wise and compelling story of becoming a mother by opening your heart. Warm, luminous and healing."
—KAREN MAEZEN MILLER, author of *Momma Zen: Walking the Crooked Path of Motherhood*

"The story of how this American samurai's kept her tender heart open in the face of continued obstacles will inspire every yogi who has ever forgotten to take refuge in their practice. Full of beauty and joy and truth and goodness and courage, this is a love story and a yoga page-turner."—CYNDI LEE, author of *May I Be Happy: A Memoir of Love, Yoga, and Changing My Mind*

"A wise and absorbing narrative of a nonconformist life. Leza Lowitz writes with spirit and clear vision. I admire the book as I admire the life."—LEONARD GARDNER, author of *Fat City*

"A poignant, inspirational, and moving 'Made in Japan' love story that demonstrates the power of persistence and never giving up on your dreams."—WENDY TOKUNAGA, author of *Love in Translation*

"Lowitz's adoption of Japan's mothering customs, coupled with values from her own Jewish background, make *Here Comes the Sun* a wise, fascinating, and deeply intelligent read."—LIANE WAKABAYASHI, writer and creator of *The Genesis Way: Making Art through Intuition*

"Before reading Leza Lowitz's memoir *Here Comes the Sun*, I knew nothing about yoga. But her engaging writing hooked me. Now, I'm intrigued. What I do know about is adoption. And the story of how Leza opened her heart to become mother to her son touched me deeply."—JESSICA O'DWYER, author of *Mamalita: An Adoption Memoir*

"This is a book about opening—opening the body, the mind, the heart. Opening to possibility. To wonder. To forgiveness. To love. The sunlight Leza Lowitz creates in these pages is like a smile that glints deep inside the ribcage, then spreads and spreads until it can't help but radiate out of every cell."—GAYLE BRANDEIS, author of *Fruitflesh: Seeds of Inspiration for Women Who Write*

"*Here Comes the Sun* proves that love is not bound by blood. I highly recommend it to anyone interested in that which connects us, holds us together, and makes us family."—MC YOGI

"Japan is a country where the cherished old ways are being shaken and sifted. Instead of blind obedience to social mores, young people are now asking 'Why?' Yet releasing outdated social mores will result in a weakening of society and individuals if there is nothing to put in their place. Leza Lowitz and her husband Shogo offer something: the impetus of heartfelt desire and the personal courage to carry it through. An inspiring story to all, Japanese and otherwise, who contemplate 'bucking the system'—teaching us that love and joy are our companions on that hard road."—REBECCA OTOWA, author of *At Home in Japan*

"In this beautiful and moving memoir, Leza Lowitz captures the ache we all have for love, and how the purest search can take us to unexpected corners of the earth. Her story had so much for women of our age to relate to, and I cheered as I read of her search for a child—the spirit of the child she karmically knew was out there waiting for her, a spirit which did not give up—and neither did she. I loved the romance, and her depiction of a couple's life lived across two countries, and the founding of her yoga studio—Lowitz is a pioneer. As I read, I re-examined my own life, and I finished her beautiful book determined to try to live with the same spirit of honesty, and with a goal toward meeting the demands the outer and inner worlds place upon us. I was deeply moved by Lowitz's effort to continue to search for so many different kinds of truths."—MARIE MUTSUKI MOCKETT, author of *Where the Dead Pause, and the Japanese Say Goodbye*

"*Here Comes the Sun* is completely captivating. Leza Lowitz offers many gifts in this very personal narrative, including absolute candor about her journey to create a family in Japan against great odds. Lowitz writes with verve and insight and shows us what it's like to forge a full and glorious life in another country, though not without trials that test her remarkable spirit. I truly relished every page."—ELIZABETH MCKENZIE, author of *Stop That Girl* and *The Portable Veblen*

Here Comes the Sun

A Journey to Adoption in 8 Chakras

Leza Lowitz

Stone Bridge Press · Berkeley, California

Published by
Stone Bridge Press
P.O. Box 8208, Berkeley, CA 94707
TEL 510-524-8732 · sbp@stonebridge.com · www.stonebridge.com

Grateful acknowledgment is made for permission to quote from the following:

America and Other Poems: Selected Poetry by Ayukawa Nobuo by Nobuo Ayukawa. Translated by Shogo Oketani and Leza Lowitz. Published by Kaya Press. ©2007 Shogo Oketani and Leza Lowitz.

Sacred Sanskrit Words: For Yoga, Chant, and Meditation. Published by Stone Bridge Press. ©2004 Leza Lowitz and Reema Datta.

Yoga Poems: Lines to Unfold By by Leza Lowitz. Published by Stone Bridge Press. ©2000 Leza Lowitz.

Printed in the United States of America.

10 9 8 7 6 4 3 2 1   2019 2018 2017 2016 2015

LIBRARY OF CONGRESS CATALOGING-IN-PUBLICATION DATA
Lowitz, Leza.
 Here comes the sun : a journey to adoption in 8 chakras / Leza Lowitz.
   pages cm
 p-ISBN 978-1-61172-021-1 (paperback)
 e-ISBN 978-1-61172-913-9 (e-book)
 1. Lowitz, Leza. 2. Authors, American—20th century—Biography. 3. Yoga.
4. Motherhood. 5. Adoption—Japan. I. Title.
 PS3562.O8963Z46 2015
 811.54—dc23
 [B]

                              2015006225

for Peggy

"One does not discover new lands without consenting to lose sight of the shore for a very long time."

—André Gide, *The Counterfeiters*

But wherefore do not you a mightier way
Make war upon this bloody tyrant, Time?
And fortify your self in your decay
With means more blessed than my barren rhyme?
Now stand you on the top of happy hours,
And many maiden gardens, yet unset,
With virtuous wish would bear your living flowers,
Much liker than your painted counterfeit:
So should the lines of life that life repair,
Which this, Time's pencil, or my pupil pen,
Neither in inward worth nor outward fair,
Can make you live yourself in eyes of men.
  To give away yourself keeps yourself still,
    And you must live, drawn by your own sweet skill.

—Shakespeare, Sonnet 16

CONTENTS

11   *About the Chakras and This Book*

13   *Prologue*

17   FIRST CHAKRA : MULADHARA

49   SECOND CHAKRA : SVADHISHTHANA

91   THIRD CHAKRA : MANIPURA

107   FOURTH CHAKRA : ANAHATA

127   FIFTH CHAKRA : VISHUDDHA

151   SIXTH CHAKRA : AJNA

179   SEVENTH CHAKRA : SAHASRARA

193   EIGHTH CHAKRA : SOUL STAR

258   *References*

260   *Acknowledgments*

ABOUT THE CHAKRAS AND THIS BOOK

This is not a story about navigating the ins and outs of adoption in a foreign country. It is about navigating the ins and outs of my own body and spirit to heal, and to arrive at a place where mother-hood could become a possibility. I've taken the chakra system as a metaphor and roadmap for personal growth and transformation, charting the movement from "me" to "we."

The word *chakra* comes from the Sanskrit root *car* "to move." It also means "wheel," "circle," "center," "disc," "sphere." In this system, there are seven major wheels of energy in the human body. The body has a central channel of subtle energy, the *sushumna nadi*, which runs inside the spine, and two other channels of energy running to the right of the spine (*pingala nadi*) and on the left (*ida nadi*). Six chakras are located at the points where these channels intersect with the central channel. The seventh chakra is at the crown of the head. The eighth chakra is believed to be our auric field.

Each chakra has a particular consciousness and function. It regulates, distributes, and balances the energy and nerve functions of its location. It has an associated color, mantra, gem, and sound. Each chakra has an "enlightened" (unblocked) and "unenlight-ened" (blocked) state.

When the chakras are blocked, the energy is choked at each point, creating imbalance. Unblocked, the *kundalini shakti* is unbound from the base and the energy flows freely. Life is in harmony and we are embodying our full potential.

Just as antennae pick up radio waves and transform them into sound, chakras pick up energetic vibrations and distribute them through the body. When this powerful energy is awakened through yoga, it moves from the right and left channels, where we have thoughts of aversion and attachment, into the central channel, where we're content and whole. Along the way, it hits the chakras, untangling the blocks at these "choke points" so that the energy can rise up to the crown. There, *shiva* (male) and *shakti* (female) energy meet, harmonizing the yin and yang. We become awakened, unified, whole.

Some chapters of this book deal directly with a particular chakra and the yogic practices that helped to balance it. In others, the work is more symbolic.

Across inner and outer oceans, the chakras have guided my journey, underscoring a simple truth I might have previously dismissed: *Sometimes you have to travel a very great distance to find a home within yourself.*

Prologue

Ma, 1999

I'm standing at a crepe stand in Harajuku, about to order the chocolate fudge whipped cream special drizzled with strawberry sauce, just decadent enough to take away the misery. The girl in front of me wears a fringed vest, tie-dyed T-shirt and patchwork jeans. Her clothes are vintage seventies; she reminds me of myself as a teenager, but she's old enough to be my daughter. Behind her is a young mother in a pastel-colored blouse, pleated skirt, shiny pumps—pristine to a fault, though her kids are running amok. She recalls my mother in the early 1960s, dressed in perfect Talbots and pearls, with my two sisters and me in tow. I stand between the women, considering. Daughters and mothers. I've been one for thirty-seven years; will I ever be the other?

Before I had a child, I wanted to have a strong, solid relationship.

I wanted to establish my career.

I wanted to see the world.

I wanted to heal my relationship with my family.

And last but not least, I wanted to find myself.

Like many women of my generation, I wanted to have it all. And I was willing to go pretty far to make it happen—like moving all the way across an ocean to Japan. But now I'm at a standstill, eating a crepe in the land of Hello Kitty, and wondering how I got here.

"*Kirei*—pretty," the seventies girl says, eyes resting on my garnet choker. I touch the stones. Garnet—from the Latin word *granatum*, for pomegranate—the fruit Persephone ate in the underworld. It's a symbol of the sacred feminine chalice, the womb. The necklace has a story. My womb has a story, too, one yet untold. But now I have a hint from Dietmar, a psychic I've just visited at a nearby salon. And I have what I *really* need—hope.

He'd looked up from the Tarot cards, shaken the black curls from his eyes.

"Where's your son?" he'd asked.

"What son?" I replied, though I knew the answer, as did he. My son wasn't here.

"I see the soul of your child. He wants to come in. You and Shogo are supposed to have a child," he'd said.

Supposed to? Wasn't that presuming a lot?

"How? When? Where?" I'd replied.

"How should I know?" He'd waved his hands, turning over another one of his crazy Keith Haring Hermès cards.

"Well, you're the psychic. You're supposed to know things like that," I'd laughed.

"No. That's your journey. To figure it out," he'd said evenly, flipping the card back. He'd known me for five years, knew how to get to me.

"I'm working on it."

"Maybe you should stop working so hard," he'd said, smiling.

"I would if I could," I'd sighed.

Working hard had become my normal. Juggling three jobs to pay the bills, using my "free time," to write a gazillion drafts of a novel that still wasn't finished. I had carpal tunnel and nothing to show for it. Things weren't going particularly well.

I wanted to give up the struggle. If I stopped trying, though, I believed that nothing would happen at all.

But the fact that he had seen a child in my future was encouraging, and I hung onto those words as I left the salon and tried to weave my way through the crowded street, tried to find the empty spaces. I was living in California now and was not used to the crush.

In Japan, there's a word for empty space, like the white around a haiku on the page, the blank canvas on the top of a scroll of calligraphy, or the void between rocks in the ocean where sacred rope is strung. It's called *ma*, written as the sun seen through a gate. It is also the universal name for Mother.

Ma . . .

In my body, the center was empty when it should have been full.

By the time I got back to the house where I was staying, my head was spinning. I wanted to shut off the chatter. Yoga offered me that, at least for a time.

I unrolled my mat, lay down on my back. I deepened my breath. I started to move my spine—stretching, twisting, feeling into my body. I hugged my knees into my chest and rocked up to standing. I put my feet together in Mountain Pose, spread my toes, and breathed down into my pelvis. I tried to feel a strong foundation within me, to find the roots that might reach down to the ground from my core, connecting me to something bigger than myself. I swept my arms over my head in a Sun Salutation, moving with my breath. As I rose skyward, I felt taller, freer, bigger than my worries. As I dived down, I felt more tethered to the earth. My body warmed with a fire that seemed transformative. I softened, surrendered.

Was this what Dietmar was talking about? Was there a different kind of surrender than "giving up"?

I'd learned that yoga helped us change ourselves, helped us change our responses to that which we could not change. As I moved through my practice, I hoped that it might help me make the emptiness a fullness, too.

Muladhara

FIRST CHAKRA

From the Sanskrit term for "root" or "support." The root chakra is located at the base of the spine, where the *kundalini shakti*—the divine feminine cosmic energy—is coiled. This chakra is considered the center of physical and material existence, health, survival. The element is earth.

When the first chakra is balanced, we feel grounded, stable, secure, connected to our bodies and able to stand on our own two feet. We are able to survive and thrive.

Free Jazz, 1993

June is rainy season in Japan. Typhoons often hit this season, and this summer day is no exception.

I'm sitting inside my studio apartment in Shibuya, watching the rain pelt down outside. I've lived in Tokyo for the past four years, made my home in the first floor of an old wooden house amidst the skyscrapers and apartment complexes. Twice destroyed—once by an earthquake in the 1920s, next by American firebombs in the 1940s—the city was thrown up hastily, with little regard for beauty. Only a few temples and old wooden houses dotted the crooked back alleys, throwbacks to a simpler time. But it's the back alleys that I love. It's on one that I live, alone.

I have no children to take care of, no spouse to consider. I teach English at a university, write book reviews and an occasional feature. I go to the gym, meet friends for dinner, or not. I kick my heels off and plop down on the futon, open a book or magazine. My life is mine.

As the rain pours down outside, I open the paper. My horoscope says the planets are aligned once this way every two hundred years, and that whatever happens today, *whatever*, I should say YES.

I fold the newspaper up. Even if the planets know something I don't, there's no way I'm going anywhere in this downpour.

But Wadada, an American musician friend, calls. He invites me to a jazz bar half an hour from Tokyo in Yokohama, where he's playing that night. I want to say no, but I remember what the planets are doing, and I wonder if this is the thing I am supposed to say "yes" to. I invite my friend Beth, who says she'll go.

By the time I get to the dark bar an hour later, my umbrella is in tatters, my clothing is drenched, and the set has already started. Wadada is playing trumpet, and a man named Sabu is playing drums. Beth's inside, waiting. She's a tall, blonde American who's fluent in Japanese. She works at a major publishing house and probably has a million deadlines, yet she's come out in a typhoon. I admire her spirit. I take a seat next to her, order a drink.

"Thanks for coming out," I say.

She nods, raises her glass. We clink them together, say *kanpai*.

The music sounds like giant boulders crumbling as the world breaks apart. A red light from someone's tape recorder blinks nearby, capturing the escalating rhythms. A woman talks too loudly to the bartender. A man smokes a pipe, its trail billowing around the chaotic sounds of the jazz. Beth and I look at each other. We're in for a long night.

Then I look past her and see a Japanese guy sitting against the wall across from us, slowly smoking a cigarette. His eyes are half-closed: he seems to be concentrating deeply. He has short black hair, smooth olive skin. He's wearing a polo shirt, canvas deck shoes without socks, and jeans. He's cute, but way too young for me. And what's a preppy doing in a dive bar listening to free jazz?

I light up, too. When I look over at the man across from me, he inhales deeply. I burn a stare into him the next time I take a drag. He holds my gaze back, inhales. We do this a few times. I'm not really a smoker, but it takes my mind off the music. I enjoy our wordless conversation in the plumes. It's very direct, and feels very un-Japanese.

When the music ends, I tell Beth I'm going over to talk to him.

"Really? You don't even know him," she whispers.

"That could change," I say, more boldly than I feel.

Beth nods, rolls her eyes. I go up to his table. He pulls out a chair.

"Thanks for coming over," he says in English. We talk about the music, the rain, California, Japan. It's easy. His forehead doesn't break into a sweat. He doesn't stammer or suck in big breaths like some Japanese men I've met. He just talks. Normally.

"You're unusual for a Japanese guy," I say.

He smiles shyly.

"I don't like to think of myself as a Japanese. I like to think of myself as a human being," he replies.

I nod. That is always a good idea. And it's something I forget here, as a foreigner, where I often let my "foreignness" define me.

His name is Shogo, which he tells me means "self-reflection." He's named after the protagonist of a novel about the burgeoning student movement. I tell him I know a bit about that, being from Berkeley. I tell him I know Wadada.

He says he writes poetry and knows Sabu. He's just published his first book of poems, about jazz. I tell him I'm a writer too, even though I've not yet published a book.

The club gets hot, and Shogo rolls up his sleeves, showing his muscles. He does it in a shy way that seems sweet rather than obnoxious. But it makes me laugh.

His arms are thin, toned. He says he does karate.

Across from us, Beth gets up. I signal for her to come over, but she waves her hand. The rain's let up, and it's a good time to leave. I give Shogo my *meishi*, my calling card. As is customary, he gives me his in return. We bow politely and say goodbye.

It's almost midnight, time to catch the last train home.

Bad Date

Over the next few weeks, Shogo calls a few times. Somehow I'm never home when he calls, so he leaves messages, says he'll call again. He doesn't leave his number, and I don't call him back. He feels a little too good to be true. A few weeks go by, and he stops calling. I notice that I miss the calls.

My aunt Peggy calls me from California, asks if I want to go on a date with a friend's nephew, a lawyer working in Tokyo for a big law firm. She hasn't met him and cannot vouch, but I have nothing to lose. I meet him for dinner. He seems nice enough, but says he hasn't been very good to women and wants to change. In fact, he's been kind of a jerk, he confesses. The revelation makes him feel better, but makes me feel worse. I'm glad he's trying to deal with his intimacy disorder, but I don't feel the chemistry. And I don't want to take on a project—I've had enough of those kinds of men in my life.

We go to a bar called Tantra, have a drink. Then, I say we should call it a night, but I'm thinking that maybe I'll call it a night on relationships in general. It's pretty clear that if Mr. Right is out there, I haven't found him. To be honest, I'm not sure if I've really found myself.

At 3 a.m. I stand in my doorway with Mr. Tantra. My phone rings. Didn't I turn my answering machine on?

"It seems urgent. I think I should go," I say, happy to wiggle out of the awkward lips-or-cheek dilemma we're on the threshold of.

I wave goodbye and close the door behind me, turning the double locks. I pick up the phone and take it to my bedroom, sliding the *fusuma* door behind me.

"Hello? Hello?" a voice says, sounding slightly drunk.

"Shogo?"

"Uh-huh. It's me," he says, laughing shyly.

"Do you have any idea what time it is?" I look around, hoping the ringing hasn't woken up the neighbors. We do live practically on top of each other.

"Yeah. But I knew you were up."

"How do you know this?" I ask, not sure I want to know.

"I just knew," he says.

Has he been calling me all night, waiting for me to pick up?

He clears his throat. "So anyway, how are you?"

"Well, I'm better now. You just saved me from a horrible date," I say, laughing.

"Oh, that's good. Happy to be of service," he says. "What was he like?"

"You really want to know?"

"Sure," he says. "Why not?" I can almost see him shrug.

I tell him, and soon enough we're both laughing.

"So, am I ever going to see you again?" he asks.

"I don't know."

"At least that's not a *no.*"

I laugh. It's not a yes, either.

He doesn't push it. Instead, he changes the subject, tells me he's writing a column about Walter Benjamin, the Jewish literary critic who'd escaped from the Nazis but was later killed trying to leave Spain. I'm surprised he knows of Benjamin. And this makes me wonder, does he know I'm Jewish, too?

He asks me what I'm reading. I tell him Kundera, but not without hesitation, because I don't want to sound too earnest, or like a show-off. Who talks about this kind of thing at three in the morning? Then again, we could be talking about chopsticks or sushi. I settle down into the couch. I do love Kundera, the way people in his novels fall in love with each other's brains and hearts. But I don't tell Shogo that.

"How old are you?" I ask.

"Thirty-three."

"No way. You're older than me?"

I've just turned thirty, but I don't tell him, mainly because he doesn't ask. I like that.

I throw my feet up on a beanbag chair, pull a shawl across my chest, and look up to see my mother staring down at me from a photo on the bookshelf. She had three kids by the time she was thirty.

I try to focus on what Shogo's saying about Benjamin's essay on Paul Klee's drawing *Angelus Novus—Future Angel*. The angel sees the wreckage of history, wants to help humanity repair the future. But a storm forces his wings open so he can't land, and the wind blows him away before he can save the world. It's difficult to follow what Shogo's trying to say, but I'm intrigued—I don't know that many people who talk about angels, at least not people who aren't New Age dreamers.

"Do you believe in angels?" I ask.

"I'm not sure I know what they are," he says.

I nod. Still, I like the fact that artists have thought about such things, and that Shogo knows about this Jewish writer's work.

I look back up at the photograph of my mother. I think this would make her happy. She's been worried about me, wondering if I will ever settle down. Nice Jewish boys are rare in Japan, and I'm not going home any time soon.

Tokyo is mysteriously quiet in the wee hours—no cars, trains, sirens. It feels like a nice time to talk about ideas and worlds far away. I don't even notice when the sun comes up and we have to say goodbye.

One Good Man

A week later, Shogo calls again. This time we talk about his mother, who's been diagnosed with stomach cancer. He's going to move closer to his parents to help take care of her.

At least he doesn't live at home, I think. Rents are expensive, to be sure, and independence is not as highly prized as it is in the West. Still, I'm surprised how many Japanese men over the age of thirty live with their mothers. More to the point, I'm impressed that he's giving up this independence to help his mother out in hard times.

I tell him I'm going to California for the summer, to see family, try to start a novel. He asks if he can write to me. I hesitate, then say no. Because I'll have to write him back.

"Okay, then," he replies, unfazed.

"Really?" I'm used to negotiating everything in a relationship, especially private time.

"I don't want to disturb a writer at work," he says.

"But I'd like to read your poems," I say, worried I've been too dismissive.

"I'll send them to you then," he says.

When we hang up, I feel badly that I've told him not to write.

What's your problem? I want to kick myself.

A few days later, he sends me a letter anyway, written in English, along with his poetry book, *Cold River.*

Good for you, I think, *not to listen to me.* I like it that he isn't a pushover. I like the book's title, and the poems, some inspired by reggae, and I like the letter he's enclosed. Written by fountain pen in cursive, Shogo tells me of his friend Hiroshi who ran a jazz bar called AUM. Hiroshi had died of a brain hemorrhage at forty. But before he died, he'd told Shogo to "write good works and follow your heart."

So I published this book. So I'm writing to you now.

Will you see me again?

I fold up the letter, put it in my drawer. It tugs at me. He's a good man.

Am I ready for a "good man"?

I hope that going back to America will help me find out.

A M E R I C A

Married with Kids

Over the summer, I visit old friends in Northern California, now mostly married with kids. They've got minivans, lawns with swing sets, playrooms full of lead-free wooden toys, and pantries stacked with gluten-free snacks. Some of my more adventurous friends, the ones who used to live "on the edge" in places like Alphabet City in Manhattan and Bangkok, have spent months—if not years—maneuvering to buy homes in areas with good schools.

"It's not about us anymore," they explain. "It's about the kids."

"I get it," I say.

"What about you?" they ask, balancing coffee cups on their knees as their eyes dart around the room to track their kids' whereabouts.

"I'm off on my global adventure," I say.

"Have one for us," they reply, only half kidding. "You still have time."

It's true. I'm only thirty, after all. And I want to keep exploring.

After four years abroad, being back "home" is a good place to start. I'm almost a foreigner in my hometown, a visitor to my very own life.

I go back to the old, beautiful home near the Presidio in San Francisco, with a widow's watch and atrium, where my sisters Amy, Melanie, and I grew up. As I look at the brown-shingled Victorian, I remember the night our house was set on fire. The basement playroom—with its damp concrete walls and cold sidewalk-like floors where I'd held séances with the neighborhood girls—burned completely. If not for the McDonald family, whose eight children hauled buckets of water from their house to ours, the entire three-story house would have been cinders and ash.

A note was pinned to the door. A Boy Scout confessed he'd done it on a dare.

"Did anyone have reason to do this?" the fire chief asked. "Anyone have a grudge?"

"No, not that I can think of." My mother shook her head.

"Is it because we're Jewish?" I asked.

The fireman gazed down over the brim of his hat. "I doubt that, Miss," he said.

I wasn't so sure. A *mezuzah* was on the door frame. It was there to protect us. But if we'd been protected, why had our house been set on fire?

I asked my mother about this.

"Well, the house didn't burn down, so the *mezuzah* worked," she said.

To her, it was that simple. She had her faith. That was enough.

Two years later, we took the *mezuzah* off the door frame.

We were moving again.

The United States was at war in Vietnam, and our father was called to duty. He was too old to be on the frontlines but would be a psychiatrist at the Navy base in Key West, Florida—a shipping-out point for troops.

His job was to determine who was "sane enough" to fight. Young men would call him up on their way to rooftops, threatening suicide. He'd try to help them, but sometimes he couldn't. It was not a good job.

My sisters and I went to the local Lutheran school, played on the lightning rod and climbed the lighthouse overlooking the Officer's Club. Our father barbecued shark in an old oil drum in the backyard, played golf, and washed our hair with beer. Sometimes he let us drink it.

When his tour of duty was up, we drove across the country, at one point finding ourselves in the middle of a hurricane. Our suitcases were ripped off the top of the car, spilling everything onto the highway.

"Who's going out to get them?" Dad asked.

"I am!" I squealed. I ran out to collect clothes, books, and the sea pictures we'd made from shells and broken glass. I pushed against the wind.

When I made it back to the car, I was soaking wet and exhilarated.

"That was dangerous!" my mother said, glaring at my father.

My parents fought as we careened across America. And they kept on fighting.

Finally, we arrived at our new home in Berkeley, where the real storm awaited.

* * *

Berkeley was named after an Irish bishop whose philosophy advocated, in part, a denial of the reality of the material world. It was a fitting namesake for a city of rebellion that prided itself on being out of sync with the rest of the country, if not the world.

Our new house was a Mediterranean-style mansion in the Claremont district—a manicured neighborhood in the hills, complete with a tennis resort. It was the kind of house everyone thought they wanted to live in, with marble columns and floors, a backyard pool. But cold winds gusted through it, making doors slam and windows rattle. And then there was the sarcophagus, bought for a bargain and placed in our music room. I swore the ghost of that thing haunted us.

Every night our TV screens were filled with body bags, and while the war raged in Vietnam, Berkeley exploded with antiwar protests, elusive serial killers, murderous cults, and a kidnapped heiress turned backstreet revolutionary. It was a world away from the small Midwestern town where my father and mother had met in high school and fallen in love.

My sisters and I were bussed to the utopian educational experiment called Malcolm X Elementary, off Ashby Avenue. The school had originally been named after Abraham Lincoln, but the students had staged a protest demanding that the name be changed. Even though Lincoln had led the war that set the slaves free, he'd wanted to send former slaves to a colony in Liberia. We wanted a hero who wanted equality here in America. Lincoln was out, but who was in? The students nominated candidates, and a vote was held.

We wanted a hero like Malcolm. A brave woman like Harriet Tubman, or a funny man like Dick Gregory, who made people laugh at the sad and unjust state of the world.

Malcolm won. Maybe because he'd been assassinated, or maybe because he'd come up from the twin hells of the street and prison to become a prophet of the people. Or maybe because it was

Berkeley and people did not not just talk about revolution, but they lived it.

Many of the city's streets were named after great and noble men—John Muir, John Stuart Mill, the Greek mathematician Euclid. White men, that is. I hadn't considered this until Malcolm X. There were scores to be settled; fights constantly broke out.

I was short, scrawny, female, white, and Jewish, none of which was a particularly good thing at Malcolm X. I was all too aware of the color of my skin and the evils people who wore it had inflicted on those who didn't, and I was often beaten up.

Inside me a voice said, *I am tiny, I am nothing. I am less than nothing.*

But there was nowhere to hide.

My older sister Amy threw herself into studying. My middle sister Melanie turned what would have been the maid's quarters into an artist's lair—painting, hammering, creating. Books were my refuge. I traveled to Asia through the 1001 *Arabian Nights*. I bought journals at the Five and Dime and wrote gothic poetry.

With so much violence all around us, it was easy to be pulled down. The principal tried to lift us up by inviting influential speakers in to the school. People like Maya Angelou, who swept in tall and regal, the colors of the earth—reds, browns, sunsets— radiating from her tunic like a modern dashiki. Her thick booming voice sailed out over her broad-rimmed hat, entrancing us with its power.

We read *I Know Why the Caged Bird Sings*. It was beautiful and unflinching, but her gift hadn't come easily, Maya said. She told us she'd been raped at the age of eight, and when she'd told her family, the attacker had been beaten to death. After that, she'd stopped speaking. She'd turned instead to reading and writing poetry. It wasn't until a teacher introduced her to Shakespeare's

The Rape of Lucrece that she spoke again. After years of silence, she found her voice and her power.

She'd exorted us to find ours, too, to not give in to hatred, even when it seethed all around us. For the first time I could remember, the auditorium had been quiet. We were in awe.

I wrote in my journal: *If I can't change the outside, can I change the inside?*

Mom had a necklace that said, "War Is Not Healthy For Children and Other Living Things," with the name Richard T. Johnson inscribed on the back. He was from Knoxville, Tennessee, and was nineteen years old when he'd been drafted to fight in Vietnam. He'd been a football wide receiver in high school. He'd wanted to be an engineer. He was last seen near Qui Nhon in South Vietnam. His body was never found.

"He's not a hero," the school bully Rufus had glowered when I shared my report about Richard.

"No one's ever even heard of him."

Maybe that was true. No one really knew about him except for me. And his family, of course. And the people who made the necklace. But he was a hero to me nonetheless.

My teacher walked up to my desk and put her hand on my shoulders. Her hand was firm and strong.

"He's an unsung hero," she said to the class.

I thought that when I finished my report, I'd forget about Richard T. Johnson. But I didn't. For years I wrote letters to Richard, though I never mailed them. Just feeling him there in some sort of spirit world gave me something to hold onto. Everything was changing all around me. The dead never changed.

By junior high, my mother had changed into someone I barely recognized. She'd cut her long red hair into what she called "a Helen Reddy bob." She'd also stopped dyeing it to let the gray come out. She wore earth tones and shoes that made her walk as if rolling. Gone was the perky Girl Scout leader in matching separates who made Sloppy Joes and fried chicken. In her place was a woman who cooked stuffed zucchini and talked about going back to school to get a master's degree.

Our father wanted her to stay home "with the girls," but the "girls" thought Mom should go back to school, have her own life, too.

They fought a lot.

Peggy, my mother's youngest sister, encouraged her. Peggy was a social worker who dedicated her life to the welfare of children. She had none of her own. She drove a VW van and her rescued dog named Love rode shotgun. She took me to street fairs, flea markets, political rallies.

Peggy gave me *The Diary of Anne Frank* for my twelfth birthday. I marveled at how this teenage girl could be so wise, could stay so calm, locked in a tiny closet with her neighbors. She inscribed the book "*To Leza Anne*," using my middle name.

Peggy had a copy of *Bury My Heart at Wounded Knee* by her bedside. The New York Dolls were on her turntable. Her boyfriend was African-American. She wore a T-shirt that said " A Woman's Place Is At The Top" to support a group of women who were preparing to climb Annapurna. When a neighbor's house needed painting, her block threw a paint party and got the job done. They had potlucks modeled after Judy Chicago's "Dinner Party," where my aunt and her friends dressed up as their favorite women in history. She stoked a fire inside me that was independent and free.

I loved Peggy, loved being in her realm. There was just one problem. My father felt she was a bad influence, especially on my mother, whom he believed was already "free" enough.

When Peggy stopped coming over, I stopped trying to be a "good girl." I became more rebellious, and it didn't go over well.

The more I was punished, the more rebellious I became.

As I raged, a comet named Kohoutek hurtled toward the earth. It was expected to land on my birthday, promising to become the brightest object in the sky on its first visit to the inner solar system. But it broke up along the way, losing some of its luminosity. I felt dejected by this, as if it were some sort of personal affront.

Living your own life as Peggy did felt adventurous and risky. It also seemed like the only option, because if you tried to bury your dreams inside like my mother did, they eventually exploded.

One night, Mom came into my room and sat on the edge of my bed.

"It's not going to work," she said. "I've tried. But I can't stay. I told your father that."

"What did he say?"

She shook her head.

"He didn't take it well."

"Of course he didn't," I said. *Who would?*

I felt badly for my father. He was doing what he thought would keep us together, but we were falling apart.

"Here's the thing," she said. "If you suggest something's wrong with a psychiatrist, they say you're hostile, that you should work on your anger."

I nodded. Maybe Dad was right. Mom did seem angry, but then, perhaps she had a right to be. Why couldn't she go back to university? My mother and many of her friends had worked to help put their husbands through school, after all.

"So what are you going to do?" I asked.

"I'm going to keep trying." She replied. I knew it was just a matter of time.

"Come on, let's go downstairs," she said. The sun was going down. It was time for dinner.

My sisters and I set the table. Mom lit the candles and said the Sabbath prayer, shielding her eyes as she drew the light toward her body with her hands. Mom and Dad didn't talk. I watched the wax drip down the brass candlesticks.

At the turn of the century, my great-grandmother Ida had carried these candlesticks over from Russia on a boat with my grandmother Molly and her two siblings. The candlesticks were their only posessions. My mother had inherited them.

When dinner was over I cleared the table and waved my hands over the dying flames as my mother had also done, hoping more light and less fire would come into our family.

It didn't.

Eventually, my mother went back to work as a dietitian, teaching cooking to senior citizens. She went to grad school, and my parents divorced.

She moved into a tiny apartment off College Avenue with Amy, and learned to do all the things she'd missed, like driving a stick shift and balancing a checkbook. Melanie and I stayed in the haunted house with Dad, who stayed out late more and more often, sometimes not coming home at all. Melanie immersed herself in costume design. I immersed myself in pinball at Silverball Gardens, started to skip school and avail myself of certain substances. No one really noticed that I was gone, or that my grades had taken a nosedive, or that I was smoking, drinking, and hanging out with older boys who had gun racks in their cars and bags full of marijuana and other drugs.

When I turned sixteen, I'd given my father "lip" one too many times, so he threw my stuff out onto the street. As hard as we tried, it just wasn't working for either of us. By then, Amy had gone off to college, and Melanie had moved in with my mother, whose apartment was too small for another person. Peggy was in Morocco, so I started spending more time with my best friend, Helen, staying at her house.

If I kept going downhill, it was just a matter of time before I would crash and burn.

*　*　*

In my junior year, Mr. Sereno, my Social Studies teacher, gave me my first survival tool, a means of empowerment. He explained that humans were stimulus-response machines, that we had buttons other people pressed, triggering habitual responses. There was a series of "tapes" inside our brains, tapes that looped around endlessly and trapped us in their scripts, preventing us from breaking away from these prescribed lines and finding another way to be, beyond habits and conditioning.

But we *could* break out, he suggested. We could transcend these perceived limits and find our ultimate natures, which were limitless and loving.

Meditation could get us there. We just had to be open and empty our minds.

I sat cross-legged at my desk chair and tried to focus on my breath. He guided us into meditation, said to watch each thought that passed as if it were a cloud moving through the sky.

I couldn't keep up with all the clouds. It was more like a thunderstorm. My eyes shot open.

"This is useless," I said, shaking out my half-numb legs as I tried to stand up. "It doesn't work."

"You have to keep at it," Mr. Sereno replied. "It's not a quick fix, but it sure beats the alternatives."

"Like?" I asked, skeptical.

"Depression and delusion. Or drugs and alcohol."

I laughed, but something in me sat up and took notice: *He's onto me.*

I didn't want to go down that road, which would have been so easy to do, and so available already. So day after day, I sat in my little wooden desk chair, legs folded up under me, watching my breath, letting the thoughts pass like clouds.

One day, we put our chairs in a circle and talked about our meditation experiences.

"I think I'm having a nervous breakdown," I confessed.

"Maybe you are. Don't worry about it," he said.

"What do you mean, don't worry? You mean it's okay to go crazy?" I asked. Going crazy was my worst fear.

"Of course not," he said. "If you're aware of your thoughts and feelings, then you're not 'going crazy.' It's the ego, trying to hold on at all costs."

"So how do you get beyond it?" I felt as if I were being stripped bare, dying.

Mr. Sereno said we had to go to the deepest, darkest corner of the soul and sit there with ourselves. He said then we would understand the changing nature of thoughts, of everything. We would "get" that we weren't our bodies. We weren't even our minds.

We weren't our bodies? We weren't our minds? Then what were *we?* I wondered.

At Mr. Sereno's encouragement, we punched pillows and screamed into blankets to "process our feelings."

He was big on self-expression.

"If you're angry, be angry. Scream! Cry! Rant! Let it out, then let it go," he would say.

Then, when he was satisfied we could focus, he'd sit us down to meditate.

"Look, kids. It's a lifelong process. It's something you commit to every day. And then one day, you'll understand where things come from."

"Where is that?" I asked.

"From your own mind. That's the awakening. That's when you'll find peace."

I wanted peace so badly. Not the Peace Sign or the Happy Face or any of that bullshit, but real peace.

"Once you get a glimpse of the limitless realm, you can't go back," he said. "You can't walk out the door. You stay—and then you experience yourself just as you are. Not the story, not the ego, but what's behind the story."

"What's behind the story?" I was dying to know.

"The space of unity, of wholeness. Of love."

I frowned. That sounded like more of the same "Peace, Love and Understanding" party line so many hypocrites were always spouting. The ones who were tearing each other apart.

Mr. Sereno said if we stayed unconscious, we'd be nothing more than a quivering mass of external influences. But somewhere underneath it all, we had a core that was unchanging, a boundless essence connecting us to the universal energy field, to love and peace, just waiting to be unearthed. Meditation helped us tap into that place. So did yoga, Tai Chi, chanting.

Chanting? Like the Hare Krishnas banging their drums and dancing along Telegraph Avenue draped in pink sheets?

"How long will it take?" I asked.

"The realizations come from disciplined practice," Mr. Sereno assured us. "That means sitting every day, watching the contents of your mind, detaching from what arises. It could take years, or it could take lifetimes."

"Lifetimes? I don't have lifetimes."

A Cup of Japanese Tea

Over time, meditation did get easier. It gave me glimpses of another place, a quieter place to be.

And my family life had calmed down. By then, I had practically moved in with Helen's family. Her father was a professor of Russian, her mother worked at a bank. They both had careers yet somehow they made it work. Their house was always full of music and laughter; family friends constantly dropped by. Some of them were doctors planning a trip to Nepal, where they were going to open an eye clinic. They made me realize you could use your resources to do something good for others, instead of just buying more "stuff" for yourself.

Helen's mother helped me get my grades back up, talked to me about the future. She asked about my dreams and wishes.

"Do you want to be a writer?" she asked.

I said I didn't know.

"I've seen you writing in your journal. And you always have your nose in some book."

"That's true," I conceded.

"Well, you need to go to college," she said. "You're a smart girl. Don't waste it."

She sent out for college applications, and when they arrived we sat down together to fill them out. She said if I wanted to be a writer, I had to go to New York.

With her encouragement, I applied to NYU. She believed in me, so I owed it to her at least to try. If I was accepted, I'd apply for student loans and work-study. I'd work three jobs to stay in school if I had to.

If I wasn't accepted, I could say I'd given it a fair shot.

Meanwhile, my mother encouraged me to learn to type, so I could support myself as a secretary if I needed to.

And now that she was on her feet, Mom herself was more at ease. She moved to a bigger place in Rockridge. I left Helen's house and I moved in with her. She shared her studies with me, and poetry like Adrienne Rich's *Diving into the Wreck*. The title poem is about a woman who journeys into the wreck of her former life, questioning the myths that define women and those she has let define herself. In the process of exploration, she's able to surface from the ruins, claim her own body and her own life on her own terms.

She also shared with me her refuge, the Japanese Tea Garden in Golden Gate Park.

With its tranquil garden, bright-red serpent-like moon bridge over a water-lily pond, and pink cherry blossom trees, it was a more peaceful world.

We sat on the *tatami*-mat floor, crunching tiny rice crackers and drinking hot tea from a crackle-glazed pot. We watched the maple leaves float to the ground, listening to the water ripple on the pond. Mom talked about her dreams for herself, and for me.

At the nearby de Young Museum, we fired *raku* pottery in an oil drum filled with red-hot hay, retrieving the glowing pieces with long iron tongs. Even when my tea bowl turned out lopsided, my mother insisted it was beautiful the way it was.

* * *

Twenty years later, my mother and I sit in the Japanese Tea Garden, reflecting on how things have changed. Integrated schools are now the norm, working moms are everywhere. Berkeley has changed, too. It's become "gentrified" and expensive, a gourmet ghetto. But it still has a rebellious streak and is populated by plenty of people for whom the sixties never ended.

They'd ended for my mother, though. She'd remarried, to a man who adored her. They had moved up to the wine country. My father also had remarried. He and his younger wife were traveling the world. As for me, I'd gone to college and grad school, and then I'd moved to Japan.

My mother asks whether I've changed my views on marriage—I'd sworn never to get married or have children.

"I don't think so," I say.

"I'm sorry it was so hard for you girls back then. I wished I'd done some things differently. I wish I could go back and change it all."

"It was hard for you, too," I say. I'm not sure I'd change any of it. But I still hadn't found a reason to change my feeling that marriage was a trap. Families fell apart. It was best not to even go there.

"Is there anyone in your life?" she asks.

"No."

"I just want to see you happy."

Then I remember Shogo. We haven't gone out yet, but something about him has stuck with me. I tell her about him.

"He sounds lovely," she says. "Like a keeper."

A keeper. Something to hold onto. *Is this even possible?*

I check the mail for a letter, but of course, Shogo doesn't write because I'd told him not to and hadn't given him my address.

Footsteps

When summer ends, I return to Tokyo. The flight is bumpy, as are my nerves. Even though I'm looking forward to returning, the trip to California has unsettled me, and I'm unsure of what's ahead.

I go back to teaching, writing, doing what I've been doing for the past three years. I think of Shogo, wonder if he'll call. I can't find the courage to pick up the phone.

Had Professor Tokiwa been right?

In 1988, I'd gotten my master's degree in creative writing at San Francisco State and was looking for work. Jobs were few and far between, but I'd heard about a teaching gig in the Japanese countryside. I applied. At the interview, Professor Tokiwa, a traditional Japanese woman who headed up the Japanese Department, was doubtful.

"You're a strong candidate, but you're a poet . . . ," she said, hesitating.

"And so?"

"That means you'll just go to Japan and fall in love."

"What?" I was shocked. Could she say such a thing and not be sued?

"I'm not going to fall in love with a Japanese man!" I said, indignant. It was the last thing I could ever imagine.

She was not convinced.

"I'm sorry. We can't afford to take a chance," she shook her head.

The grant went to a business student. I stayed at San Francisco

State for a semester to teach composition, then set out for Japan with $500 to my name.

I taught English to businessmen, wrote book reviews for the *Japan Times*, and landed a job teaching at Todai, Japan's Harvard. Shortly after I'd moved, the teaching grants at S.F. State were axed in budget cuts.

I'd made the right choice. Had Professor Tokiwa made the right choice, too?

One night, I'm sitting in my apartment, positioned under the light of the single lamp in my *tatami* room, reading Galway Kinnell's poem "After Making Love We Hear Footsteps." I try to imagine what it would be like to be long married, to be intimate with the same person for years, and to hear your child's footsteps down the hall, to write a poem about it.

The phone rings.

It's Shogo. He's casual, as if we've just spoken yesterday, as if months hadn't passed since since we'd met in Yokohama.

He wants to know if I will go see a movie with him.

Thoughts careen into each other like bad Japlish T-shirts. *Cross-cultural relationships are doomed to fail.* And this, from my childhood—*A woman needs a man like a fish needs a bicycle.*

"Well?" he asks.

This time I pause.

I take a deep breath, watch the objections arise in my mind. He's not my type. He's not my race. He's not my religion, though I hardly practice it myself. He's not so many things. The thoughts come and go, passing like clouds.

Good Date, 1993

On the morning of our date, I go see my Austrian friend Edgar in Yanaka—an old section of Tokyo that remains much as it was a century ago—it wasn't destroyed by a quake or bombed in the war. The houses are wooden, traditional. The streets are narrow and crowded with temples and ateliers.

Edgar is an artist and filmmaker whose rickety apartment has purple *fusuma* doors and old *tatami* mats. There's a persimmon tree outside the window and a view of the graveyard in the nearby temple. Japanese won't live there for fear of footless ghosts.

We walk around the neighborhood—he sketches and I write. The daylight starts to wane.

"Hey, hadn't you better get going? Don't you have a date with that guy, what's his name? Shogun?"

"Shogo," I say, laughing. My feet crunch loudly along the pebbled path of the graveyard. ". . . I canceled it."

"Why?" He asks, blue eyes gazing into mine.

"I don't really know," I say, honestly. "I guess I have a lot of baggage."

He frowns, shakes his head. "Well, get over it. We all have baggage. Call him up again. I have a first date, too. I can make dinner. The four of us can hang out. Come on!"

"Nah. I couldn't do that. It would hurt his pride."

"Just try."

"It's too late. I've made my decision," I say, shaking my head.

He stops, turns to face me. "I don't want to say this, but I'm going to anyway because I'm your friend. Why do you always go for guys who treat you badly?"

"I don't," I say, hurt.

"Yes, you do."

"No, I don't," I say, like a squabbling sibling.

"Yes, you do. See how defensive you are? If you didn't, you wouldn't be so affected by what I'm saying. Shogo sounds like a nice guy."

"He is . . ."

"Just give him a chance."

I know he's right, and what do I have to lose, really? When we get back to the apartment, I make the call. To Shogo's credit, he says he'll come. Edgar cooks. We drink wine and talk about the new emperor, the new era of Heisei, or "peace everywhere." Shiori, Edgar's sexy and brilliant date, majored in French philosophy. So did Shogo. They talk, get along well. They even *look* good together.

"Perfect. The two of them can get together," I whisper to Edgar in the kitchen as we're clearing the dishes.

"No way," Edgar protests. "She's a knockout! I'm not letting her go!"

We laugh and wash the plates. After more wine and *sacher-torte*, Edgar kicks us out before the last train home.

Shogo and I walk back to the station. He talks about the neighborhood, tells me what Tokyo used to be like in his childhood. Empty lots, stray dogs, war veterans in white kimonos sitting on the street. The city was different then—before the Bubble Years in the 1980s, when the Japanese were buying everything from Rockefeller Center to multimillion-dollar Monets and van Goghs. It was quieter, fewer cars, more interaction.

Somewhere far off someone plays a *shamisen*. The twangy sound startles us in the still night air. We stop to listen. I also listen to my heartbeat, steadying my breath in my belly. One thing I learned from Mr. Sereno is that our true feelings live in the *hara*— the gut, not the head. My gut says I am happy.

I take Shogo's hand. And gently but firmly, he takes mine, too.

Not to Seek for Love

All through the fall, Shogo and I go to the movies, out to dinner, on walks.

We jog around the Imperial Palace, the former Edo Castle, with its whitewashed buildings, sloping black-tile roofs, and imposing moat. The grounds are reportedly worth the same amount as much of the real estate in California. When we finish, he lights up a cigarette.

I tell him that if he wants to be with me, he has to stop smoking. I've already quit.

He switches to a pipe. It makes him seem anachronistic, like someone out of an *Esquire* cognac ad in the sixties.

"The pipe has to go too, you know," I say.

"Just give me some time."

"Okay." I agree. He's certainly given me time to come around to him.

This kind of negotiation makes a relationship feel easy. There's no drama, no incessant "processing," which frees up a lot of time and space to just enjoy life. This comes as a revelation to a girl from Northern California, where you can spill your entire life story on a first meeting.

I begin to edit an anthology of Japanese women's poetry. The poets write about marriage, love, war, peace, divorce, regret— frankly and fiercely, leaving behind the traditional Japanese "good wife, wise mother" dictum.

I stay over at Shogo's house, and he stays over at mine. In the morning, Shogo does his karate *kata* while I do my running stretches. We jog together. We read, write, and cook together. Or rather, he cooks and I watch. He tells me that when he was grow-ing up, his mother didn't like cooking, so his sisters Ayano and Hitomi and he would watch *The Galloping Gourmet* on TV and copy the recipes. He can cook anything—from hollandaise sauce to bouillabaisse. But he hates to clean; his apartment is a mess. Lucky for him, I'm a neat freak, so I pick up his clothes from the *tatami* and hang them in his closet.

We get to know each other slowly. Eventually I ask him if he wants to know about my past relationships. He says he doesn't.

"Really? Not at all?"

"I just want to enjoy us now."

I know I should be grateful that he doesn't need to rehash the past. Yet, I can't help but worry—is he hiding something? Or is he really so engaged in the present that he doesn't care? I feel a bit unmoored without drama. Regardless, I think—I know—that I have something to learn.

Shogo's outlook on life is part Zen, part Taoist, and doesn't put much stock in complaining or *kvetching*, which might be con-sidered a Jewish birthright. He seems to just accept whatever hap-pens as it happens.

But then, a few months later, we're in the kitchen cooking dinner together (or rather, he's cooking and I'm "helping"), when he suggests we move in together. I say I don't want to live with anyone for a while—if ever.

"Why not?" he asks.

"I'm not sure."

"I think you are," he presses.

"Well," I say, "I'm afraid one day I'd wake up and wonder where my own life went. That's what happened to my mom. I don't want that to happen to me."

"I don't think that would happen with us," he says.

"Why not?"

"Because you already have your own life. And just because we're together doesn't mean we own each other."

He mixes miso paste and butter to put with the sliced onions into scooped-out eggplant, wraps the eggplant shells in foil, and wipes his hands on his jeans.

"Think about it, okay?"

"I will."

"Great."

I think my answer has satisfied him for now, but I can tell he's just reconfiguring his plan of attack. In his mind, we're meant to be together, and when I come to my senses, we will be. It's just that simple.

I mull it over. *Could I be myself with him? Could we both grow and evolve over time?*

We sit down to his meal.

Eating it together, I feel blessed and grateful.

Back in my apartment later that night, I brush my teeth, look at the Rumi axiom I've taped to my mirror:

> *Your task is not to seek for love, but merely to seek and find all the barriers within yourself that you have built against it.*

I see now that there are many barriers. Still, Shogo's calm wisdom is like a wall of *ma* that breaks them down. He doesn't try to change me. He just gets out of my way and lets me be me. He's a mirror that throws all my objections—all my petty little fears and reactions—back at me. And then they start to fade.

Little by little, the barriers fall.

Before I know it, he's quietly swept me off my feet.

Home Again, 1994

After four years in Japan, however, I'm burnt out from working on Tokyo time, which is really 24/7—jobs faxed at all hours, free-lance requests with impossible deadlines, getting up at 4 a.m. to teach morning classes out in the suburbs, riding packed commuter trains to get there. I've managed to save some money, but my body is run down. I'm exhausted, and I yearn for Northern California. I miss the open space, the relaxed vibe, slower pace. I miss clean air, and a certain West Coast energy I feel so far away from.

I'm eating dinner with Shogo at our favorite Italian trattoria on a particularly hot, humid day when I break the news.

"I think I need to go back home," I say softly, bracing myself for some kind of protest.

"To California?" Shogo looks up at me, halfway into tearing apart a piece of bread. He dips it into the little bowl of olive oil, then looks up again.

I nod.

Is he startled that I still don't consider Japan "home"? That I haven't put down roots in this country yet?

"You sound pretty sure," he says.

"I think I am."

"Well, in that case, okay," he says, nonplussed.

"Okay? Really?" I'm convinced there has to be more to it than that.

"Yes, really. If you're not happy, you can't force yourself to be happy."

"Do you really think that?"

"Actually, yes. If you stay here, you won't be happy. And if *you're* not happy, *we* can't be happy together. So you should go home. If we're meant to be, we'll find a way."

I smile. I think this is a beautiful thing to say. But while I admire his wisdom, it's not what I really *want* him to say. I want him to hold onto me. To fight for me. Because deep down, I realize: I want to hold onto *him*.

I twirl my pasta around my fork. He watches me eat. Then I understand. He's being *Japanese*. Restrained.

But I'm not Japanese, and I don't have to hold back. I come from a tribe for whom self-expression is almost a birthright.

"Right. Well, if it's meant to be, maybe one day we can even get married," I say, surprising myself.

"Married?" His eyes widen.

"That's what I said," I reply, not really believing it myself.

"Okay," he repeats calmly, but I can tell my words make him happy. Still, I think all that is a long way off.

He leans over the table and kisses me.

I look around, scandalized. Kissing in public is still rare in Japan, let alone in a small restaurant where everyone can see you.

As the weeks go by, neither of us brings up the subject again.

But once I've made the decision to return to the States, it becomes harder to negotiate being in Japan—the language issues, the cultural rigidity, the ambiguity, the inability to get things done as quickly as I imagine I could do them in California.

When the day comes to say goodbye, Shogo takes me to the airport.

We don't say *sayonara*.

We say *gokigenyo*. Shogo says it means "farewell."

What it really means, I learn, is *we'll meet again*.

Svadhishthana

SECOND CHAKRA

From the Sanskrit term meaning "sweetness." It also translates as
"one's own place," "base," or "support of life." The second chakra,
or sacral chakra, is located at the spleen, the center of creativity and
sexual energy, survival, and the fulfillment of physical needs. The
element is water.

When this chakra is balanced, we let our emotions flow freely, are open
to intimacy and able to accept and even welcome change.

Room of My Own, 1995

In December I rent a small studio apartment in downtown San Francisco, settle back in. But part of me stays in Japan. I keep bowing, even when talking on the telephone. I cover my mouth when I laugh. I do all the things in America that used to drive me crazy in Japan. And the things I longed for over there—direct communication and bold opinions—now sometimes feel overwrought, even confrontational here.

I call Peggy, who's now married to a feisty defense lawyer she met through work. They're planning to move to the South Bay and build a house near the ocean, and have just bought a plot of land. She's still doing social work, still seeing her Berkeley friends, still on a grand adventure.

I tell her I feel rootless, unbound, that I don't know where "home" is anymore. She suggests I might have reverse culture shock, and that it's perfectly normal. Japan is so different, and I've been away for a while. I'm different, now, too.

I know that in order to readjust I have to first adjust. My out-of-sync life has become so habitual that I don't even notice it might not fit anymore, like a pair of beloved but outgrown shoes.

Luckily, I can freelance for a Japanese publisher and fax the jobs back to Tokyo. In my free time I write, take hikes in the Marin Hills, comb the aisles at City Lights bookstore, and wait for the days to pass until I can see Shogo again. He's planning to visit in February. After the New Year's holiday and subsequent busy-ness has subsided.

When I meet him at the San Francisco Airport, he looks shy,

nervous even. He's only been abroad once before, when he was eighteen and his father took him to Paris on an eighteen-hour flight with a steamer trunk. I've seen the photos: Shogo in three-piece suits in fancy restaurants with way too many knives and forks set out in front of him, or in front of gilded museums holding his father's leather satchel, looking formal and miserable.

This is going to be a stretch, I think, looking at him now. *For both of us.*

And he hasn't met my family yet.

When meeting your girlfriend's family, you can't arrive empty-handed. Not if you're Japanese. Shogo had asked me what my father wanted from Japan. I tell him he really doesn't have to bring anything, but Shogo insists. So I ask my father what he wants. He requests a sake barrel. Not full, but empty, for decoration—to use as a coffee table or foot stool or god knows what.

He wants a basket-type barrel covered with bamboo wrapping, and Shogo wants to please my father, so he goes out of his way to find a special one with a beautiful label from a brewery in the countryside. He has it shipped down to Tokyo, then he carries it on the plane. He's holding it when I pick him up.

The Sake Barrel

When my father comes to get us at the BART station, he's brought my six-year-old half-sister Barbara along in the minivan. He and Shogo make small-talk as we drive through the leafy streets of Danville to Barbara's preschool. We're an hour early, so we play on the swings until school starts, then drop her off.

When we get home, my stepmother runs out of the house.

"Where have you been? Where's Barbara?" she screams.

"I took her to school," my father says.

"What? You did what?" Nancy asks, looking past Shogo to where my father is standing, confused.

Shogo's holding the sake barrel in his outstretched hands, waiting for someone to relieve him of it.

"Let's go inside," I say, pushing him toward the door, toward Nancy so that I can introduce them properly.

"Nancy, ummm. This is Shogo. . . ." I say, putting my body between them.

She shakes her head, not hearing. And not seeing, either. He could as well be invisible.

"It's not just the first day of school. It's the first day of the rest of her life. She'll be leaving us before we know it!" Nancy says.

I shoot Shogo a look. He bites his lip, opens his mouth, then closes it. Of course, there are no words for such an occasion in the English-language textbooks. No words for meeting your girlfriend's high-strung parents for the first time.

We shuffle past Nancy, go inside. The rain slams down, just as it did when we first met at the bar in Yokohama.

Shogo hands my father the sake barrel and bows.

"This is for you, Father," he says.

My father takes it in both hands, still looking at Nancy, bewildered.

"Do you like it?" I prompt.

"It's nice," my father says, ". . . but it's not really what I wanted."

He takes the barrel and puts it down in front of the door outside. In the rain.

Shogo's very quiet. Perhaps he's thinking: *How are we going to get through the afternoon? The rest of our lives?*

Shogo looks at me and laughs.

"Oy vey," he says in his best Japanese-Yiddish accent.

I laugh, too, relieved.

My father and Nancy argue in the kitchen while we sit in the living room. The fireplace is lit, and it's warm and dry.

My father makes barbeque with every kind of meat known to mankind, even though I've been a vegetarian for years. He pours his heart into the cooking, and Shogo eats appreciatively. My father gives me a bouquet of roses from his garden—yellow, lavender, red, with thorns like little rhinoceros horns that jut from their stems. On the train back to San Francisco, Shogo turns to me.

"I'm sorry," I say.

"You don't need to see them for a while if you don't want to," he says.

"I know. I just keep hoping. . . ." My voice trails off. "You know the word *meshugenah*?"

"I think I'm about to learn."

We laugh together. I lean my head on his shoulder as we ride through the BART tunnel under the Bay.

J A P A N

The House of Dreams

I go back to Tokyo to meet Shogo's family, fully expecting they will reject me. But that's not what happens at all.

"We're happy he's found someone," Kyoko, Shogo's mother, says. "We'd given up."

He didn't tell me that his parents had suggested an *omiai* meeting with a potential marriage partner. He'd refused.

"I'm glad you met each other. *Go-en ga arimashita*," Kyoko says. *Go-en*. Destiny.

This is no small thing for her to say. As a fifth-grader, she'd been sent to the countryside to live for two years during World War II. When she returned, she saw her entire neighborhood fire-bombed by American B-29 warplanes. She and her mother had run to the nearby safe haven—the woods behind the local shrine—with their neighbors, but her mother fell down, and a voice told them to turn around. They returned home, and the woods were hit. All the others died, but Kyoko and her mother survived.

She'd met Shogo's father through her younger sister's friend, and they married. Shogo was their first child. In childhood he'd read books about America and watched American TV shows like *Leave It to Beaver*, listened to Western rock'n'roll. By the time Shogo himself was in the fifth grade, America was no longer the enemy. Many considered it Japan's "big brother."

Kyoko says that really, it's not surprising that Shogo met an American girl and fell in love. It's more surprising, she said, that I fell in love with him.

I think so, too.

And it's *my* family who's probably disappointed. They might have hoped I'd settle down with a nice Jewish guy, not a quiet Japanese atheist you had to work a little bit to talk to. I never thought I'd end up with a Japanese man, either. But I knew what I *didn't* want, and that was *someone like me*.

I wanted to break the pattern set by my parent's marriage. If I ever got married, I wanted my marriage to work. Or at least, I wanted to try to stack the deck in its favor.

Kyoko wants to honor us. She wants to do the tea cere-mony—a special, meditative sharing of green tea, *matcha*—in her teahouse in the garden, which she's named The House of Dreams. The teahouse was hand-built in the traditional style, using four different kinds of wood and no nails. It's close to nature, almost like being outside, she says. All the sounds are amplified. In the rainy season, the frogs croak loudly, calling for a mate. In the summer, the cicadas cry until they die. On humid days, mosquitoes feast. And in winter, spiders spin their webs.

It's springtime, so the weather is mild, and the cherry tree that hangs over the teahouse is flush with beautiful pink petals. They fall like rain outside the window.

The entryway is a small square door—a *nijiriguchi* ("crawl-in entrance"). You have to crouch down and crawl to get through it. In feudal times, samurai had to take off their long swords, too. All who enter the teahouse must bow, showing humility.

I'm nervous that I'll knock over the boiling water or break an expensive teabowl. I tell her this. She just laughs.

"It's just a teabowl," she says.

On the day of the ceremony, Shogo's middle sister Ayano suggests we bring in a chair so that I'll be more comfortable

"I'm not doing the tea ceremony seated on a chair," I protest. I say I'll sit on the *tatami* like everyone else. I don't tell her I used to meditate and can sit comfortably on the floor—it's been years since I've meditated, though. I wonder if I can still do it.

And so we crawl one by one into the teahouse, where we sit on bent knees on the *tatami*. All eyes are on Kyoko's movements as water drips from a fountain outside.

Each turn of the whisk, each placement of a cup or ladle is graceful, beautiful.

I look over at Shogo's father sitting stiffly; Ayano and her younger sister Hitomi are formal and expectant. It's the first time they've been in the teahouse together.

This is usually Kyoko's domain, her refuge. Just as the Japanese Tea Garden had been my mother's. I feel calm and at home here, the way I felt so many years ago there.

Kyoko places a round, pink, Japanese sweet on a plate in front of me, shaped like a cherry blossom flower. I place it in my mouth. Then I take the teabowl in my palm, turn it like Shogo does, and sip the bitter tea as I hold the sugary sweet on my tongue. The tea is hot, and the sweetness melts into the bitterness, washing it away. I sip the last drop, then turn the bowl around to admire it. It's an earthy *bizen-yaki* bowl she's chosen for me. It's brown, mottled, and slightly lopsided.

I wait quietly as each member of Shogo's family drinks their tea, admires their chosen bowl.

Then Kyoko places both hands in front of her on the *tatami*, makes a triangle with her slender fingers, and bows, her forehead resting on the floor between her hands.

I bow low in return. I thank her for opening up her world to me, thank her for giving us her blessing, thank her for giving me her son.

Go-shujin Sama

"Are you going to marry Shogo?" my friend Tomoko asks one day a few months later. She's one of the poets in the anthology I'm editing. I've been filling her in on the saga.

"I don't know," I reply. "He hasn't really asked me. And I haven't really asked him either."

"Well, everyone should get married once," she says, "otherwise you're not entitled to get a divorce."

I laugh at the statement, because it so embodies my own feelings and fears. For it's marriage I fear more than anything. Anything, that is, except divorce.

Tomoko is married. Happily, for the most part, to a professor of philosophy with whom she travels often to Europe. She's a professor of English and writes poetry in English because it does not bind her the way she feels her native language does. She has one daughter.

She's nervous about my talk of marriage for two reasons: The first is that a dedicated "bachelorette" is considering marriage at all. The second is that to her, the combination of an American feminist and a Japanese man spells trouble. I'm surprised. I don't consider myself a "feminist." Or a "bachelorette" either.

"Would you have to call him 'Master—Go-shujin sama?'" Tomoko asks, biting her lip.

"I don't know," I say. "It definitely sounds weird. What do you call your husband?"

"Anata. Darling," she says, blushing.

"That doesn't sound much better," I reply.

She twists her lip. I hope I haven't hurt her feelings.

"If we ever got married, would I have to call you those names?" I ask Shogo later.

"You think too much," he replies.

"I don't want a master. I want to be my own master," I say.

"Then do. This is your life," he says.

Those words stay with me when I return to San Francisco a week later. I miss Japan, and I miss Shogo. Being here alone makes me wonder: What is my life? And where is it?

I don't think about marriage again until Shogo's mother's stomach cancer returns a few months later. It's stage four, and this time there's no hope for recovery.

I decide to sublet my apartment in San Francisco and return to Tokyo. Shogo and I will share the two-room tatami-mat studio where he now lives. He'll go to work while I go to the hospital to be with his mother. I can pick up freelance work at my old companies and stay afloat somehow.

So I pack up and return to Tokyo, again.

Shogo's mother asks from her hospital bed what we're going to do for a *kekkon-shiki*. I mistake the word for *shikibuton*, a fluffy blanket used as the topmost layer on a futon.

"What are we going to do about a blanket?" I ask Shogo.

He smiles. "*Kekkon-shiki.* Marriage ceremony."

"Ah, that," I say, stalling.

But my mistake is not wholly innocent.

If Shogo and I ever do marry, I think, *we would probably hide under a blanket to do it.* I certainly would prefer the privacy and comfort of a *shikibuton* to the formal display of the Japanese wedding—an expensive affair full of toasts and speeches held at chapels or hotel ballrooms. The bride has to wear a formal white kimono and hat to hide her "horns of jealousy." Then she changes to a puffy Cinderella-type dress you wouldn't be caught dead in at your worst nightmare of a high school prom.

"You're on the spot now," Shogo says in English. I wonder if Kyoko understands. I look over at her. She meets my gaze. She understands. Everything.

I tell Kyoko we're thinking about it, combining the two great Japanese tactics of ambiguity and procrastination.

She accepts this answer and smiles. But it's a crafty smile, and I know that even though she's weak and ill, she's just considering another effective approach. Just like Shogo.

I tell Tomoko about the conversation. Her worries, coupled with my own, turn my feet cold.

"Would I have to be a Japanese wife? Could I still work? Would Shogo come home late, drunk, demanding a home-cooked Japanese dinner at midnight?" I ask Shogo a variation on these questions every day.

He laughs at my litany.

"Don't laugh. It happens," I say. I've heard stories. I know.

"Give me some credit," he replies.

"If we ever get married, can we live in separate apartments, like Joan Didion and John Gregory Dunne?"

Unflustered, Shogo says that would suit him fine.

Then he turns serious.

"Are you ever going to trust me? Are you ever going to see us as us, and not as your parents?"

"I don't know," I reply.

A month goes by in his little apartment, which is about as big as my bathroom in San Francisco. But I haven't once felt cramped, and we haven't fought. Not that fighting is bad, necessarily, but it's a shock to be in a serious relationship with someone I can actually talk to—and we don't even speak the same language.

Amazingly, I don't feel boxed in, even though we're sharing a rabbit hutch.

I think: *This could work*. Marriage is an agreement between adults, not a right to ownership. We're both adults, and I'm now thirty-two. He's thirty-six. Though neither of us has been married, we've been around.

His mother's condition worsens, and the question takes center stage in her life. Shogo and I sit together at her bedside. I'm holding her hand when she asks me again, flat out, if we're going to marry.

I don't answer.

"Why not?" she says as I spoon cooked pumpkin into her mouth.

"I hate the whole institution," I say.

"It takes a lot of energy to hate something. Maybe you're just scared."

"Yes," I admit. "You got me there."

"He's a good man. You're a good woman. You love each other."

"Right."

"So be happy together. Have children. Life is short."

Before Kyoko dies, we decide to take the plunge.
We go to Tiffany & Co. and buy rings.
We want to do it once, and do it right.

* * *

We marry Friday in Tokyo at the American Embassy, a simple civil service where I have to sign an "Affidavit of Competency to Marry." I do a double-take, but this is not a fluke of translation.

The certificate makes me laugh. Do we have such a certificate in America? I'd never heard of anything like it, but we must, since this is the U.S. Embassy. Just what is "marital competence" and how is it determined? Fortunately, there's no test administered, as I'd be sure to flunk it.

I raise my hand, swear to God and my country that I am competent to marry Shogo.

The paper is filed. We decide not to tell our families until after the fact. We want to start this new chapter on our own. We go out for a sushi lunch, toast each other with sake.

But we're not done yet.

Because, while I've married Shogo, he hasn't legally married me—not until we register our marriage at the Shinagawa Ward office, overseers of our district. By the time we finish our leisurely lunch, it's too late. The office is now closed for the weekend. We'll have to return on Monday.

"You still have an out," I tell him, laughing.

"You do too," he replies.

Shogo's family has a small party for us at an *udon* restaurant. His mother is frail and sick, but she is radiant. She brings me flowers that she's artfully arranged like a waterfall.

On Monday morning, Shogo and I eat breakfast together in his tiny apartment.

"Well, are we going to make it final?" he asks.

"It doesn't seem fair to leave you hanging," I say.

"Are you feeling competent?" he jokes.

"As competent as ever," I say. So we take the plunge.

But old habits die hard, and I do not take Shogo's name. This causes a commotion at the ward office. The clerk says there is no "official space" to put my own name on the form.

Shogo stands his ground. "Well, make a space," he says, knowing this is impossible. One thing about bureaucracy is that it most definitely *cannot* make a space.

I stand by and watch this exchange.

It would have been much easier for him to request, or even insist, that I change my name, but he doesn't. He just waits for the bureaucrat to find a way to remedy the situation, with a strong, quiet certainty I've grown to love.

The worker goes off to consult with his superiors. After much shuffling, air sucking, consulting with others, and whispering in the backroom, he returns with the verdict. I get to keep my own name and we can make our own *koseki*, his family register that goes back generations.

This we do.

"Welcome to Japan," Shogo tells me after we've signed and stamped all the documents and the clerk carries them off.

"Now you're official."

"In the book and everything," I add, gulping.

"Let's enjoy being *newly-wet*," he says.

I don't correct him. It seems like just the right word.

The Street of Least Resistance

It's great being newly-wet, thrown into the crazy quilt of cultural oddities that populate our days. The euphoria lasts for a while—at least until my father comes to visit a month later, wanting to meet Shogo's mother before it's too late.

We book him into a nearby hotel, but he cancels the reservation, says he wants to stay with us in Shogo's tiny apartment. I try to dissuade him, but he insists.

Kyoko's spirits lift in preparation for my father's visit. She goes to the beauty parlor. She cleans the house, puffs up pillows, wipes the *tatami*. She writes tanka poems in calligraphy on strips of Japanese paper. She looks forward to meeting him.

When he arrives, Shogo's parents take us on a boat ride on the Sumida River in Asakusa, take us to the Kannon Temple and out for sushi in the Ginza. They take him to a sake factory, and my father shines. He takes off his shoes at the right times and even remembers to bow, though his back begins to ache. He hits it off with Shogo's father. But by the third night, he's snoring so loudly that we can't sleep. Our three futons are smashed together; there's not much wiggle room. We try moving him, rolling him over to get him to stop snoring, throwing things. Nothing works.

After three sleepless nights in Tokyo, we take him to a hot springs in the wine country—Shogo's idea. *The street of least resistance*, he says.

We sit at a low table, picking at the delicate food in front of us—mysterious morsels of fish and mountain vegetables that are so intricate and precious.

After dinner, Shogo goes into the baths by himself, giving us time to talk.

My father says he wants to talk about my mother. I say I don't.

He insists, wants to explain to me, really, why things went downhill. Why she left him.

I say I think I know. It was the 1970s, it was Berkeley. They'd met in high school in the Midwest. Things changed. I get it.

"You have a wife who loves you, a child, a new life. You're happy now, right?" I say.

He orders another flask of sake. We talk some more, and he says gut-wrenchingly hurtful things I try not to take personally, which he will, of course, forget, and later deny.

I'm thankful for separate rooms, though the walls are Japanese-style and thin enough to hear him snore all evening.

The next day I'm exhausted and battered. Shogo looks at me sympathetically, but I feel sorrier for him. This isn't his idea of a honeymoon, either.

Still, he doesn't hold it against me or even my father, for that matter. He's just there for me, because he loves me. Because he took a vow to be there.

We ride the train back to Tokyo.

On the way, my father asks why I'm so angry. I'd done anger. I was over it. Now I was just tired.

"You *are* angry. Why don't you just admit it?" he presses.

I sigh. It won't make any difference what I say or don't say, I know. He'll have his version of events, and I'll have mine. It's like we're speaking different languages. Perhaps we always had been.

But mainly, I'm tired of manufacturing "crisis mode" when everything is fine.

Later that night, back at Shogo's apartment, my father snores even more loudly than before. Unable to withstand another sleepless night, Shogo and I sneak out after midnight, walking the few blocks to Shogo's aunt's house, where we spend the night.

We leave a note on the kitchen table, telling my father where we've gone. We leave the phone number so he can call when he wakes up if he wants to.

At six o'clock the next morning, he does, upset that we've "abandoned" him. He's leaving on the earliest bus to Narita Airport, going back to his "real family."

I don't try to stop him. I know there's nothing I can do.

I see him off at the airport bus, wondering when—or if—I'll see him again.

The visit makes me want to do things another way. To prove that I can be there for Shogo in whatever way he needs me. Even if it is uncomfortable, or challenging for me to go outside my comfort zone, I determine to be a good partner, a good wife. But more than that, I determine to be myself.

In the beginning, Shogo had said that we didn't own each other.

He was right.

Passing On

Shogo's mother shrinks to sixty-five pounds, though her inner strength doesn't wither. I've never sat with a dying person before. I stay with her every day, and it gets easier to be there with her, for her. Sometimes I just sit by her side, humming and holding her hand.

I feed her stewed pumpkin, wash her face, and brush her hair. She says her mother had brushed her hair when she was a child, that it brings back good memories.

Her friends and relatives come to visit, comment that I am more like a daughter than a daughter-in-law. It's easy, because I'm doing it for Shogo. It helps ease his pain.

A few weeks later, Kyoko passes away.

The funeral and memorial are a picture of Japanese formality and restraint. A funeral director and assistants come to the house and take over, bustling from room to room as they clean the house from top to bottom. Outside, special bamboo trellises and old-style lanterns are set up. Black and white silk tapestries are draped over a reception table in the *genkan*, the foyer of the home, with pens, guest books, and records for financial offerings visitors will bring when they come to pay their respects. Then there are special gifts in bags we'll give the guests to thank them for coming.

Kyoko's body is laid in state in the living room for two days. Relatives come. Friends from her childhood pay their respects; tea ceremony students, fellow teachers, and neighbors all come to say goodbye. What a beautiful person she was, inside and out, they say.

After the body is cremated, each family member picks the bones out from the ashes with long chopsticks, placing them in an urn. The bones are a glistening white, smooth and beautiful, like shells.

We take the urn to Kamakura, the medieval samurai town above the sea where Shogo's family has a burial plot. A priest blesses the ashes, and then they're buried with prior generations of ash and bone.

The sun goes down over the ocean, casting an orange glow over the hills.

It's not a bad place to end up. I wonder if I'll be buried there, too.

A few weeks later, Shogo's sisters and I go through their mother's possessions, separating out what to keep and what to give away.

They keep the Western things—the Limoges and Royal

Copenhagen and Chanel and a few silk kimonos. I keep the *wabi-sabi* rustic ceramic ware—*bizen-yaki* and mottled *hagi* tea bowls, all things imperfect and rustically Japanese. I keep the *raku* ware that reminds me of my childhood experiments, the lopsided bowl like the one Kyoko first served me tea in.

There are teacup sets, too, with the men's teacups large and the women's smaller.

"That's sexist," I say to Ayano.

"It's because women are smaller," she replies.

"But what if they're thirstier?" I ask.

"Then they go for seconds," Ayano says, laughing.

"Or they restrain themselves," Hitomi replies. I think I detect irony in her voice, but it's so subtle that it's hard to tell.

We wrap up the belongings, then go to the family altar to light incense to Shogo's mother and say a prayer. The ancestors' photos gaze down on us—Shogo's grandmother, a geisha. Now Shogo's mother—tea ceremony and flower arrangement master. Everyone is here.

Kneeling down beside them, I wonder how I will take my place in this lineage, join these generations of women. Can I fit in by being myself?

Ayano has two sons. Her husband works for one of the ministries, has gone to Japan's best university. Hitomi is single, and works as an "Office Lady." She lives with Shogo's father, and will take care of him for a while. But it's really Shogo's job, as he is the eldest son, the *chonan*.

And now it's mine.

I'm the *yome*—the bride. The daughter-in-law—written with the kanji for woman next to a house with a roof overhead:

嫁

I'm the woman of the household, even though I don't live here. And that is a very good thing, because I can't imagine how I would manage two very strong Japanese men under my roof, or how they would manage me.

CALIFORNIA

An Ocean Away

After Kyoko dies, I return to San Francisco, go back home to my apartment downtown.

I'm an ocean away from my husband, living separate lives. It's a variation on the Joan Didion/John Gregory Dunne set-up I always thought I wanted, but now that I have it, there's too much distance between us and I feel disconnected. I'd romanticized Didion, to be sure. After two years at NYU, I'd transferred to U.C. Berkeley, Didion's alma mater, and like every other female English major there, I'd idealized this literary lion. But we didn't know her really, had no idea what she struggled with in real life. I needed a living role model. I needed Peggy, the person I *did* know who came close to this type of lifestyle. When I was a teenager, my aunt had encouraged me to explore the world, to pursue a career, to get to know myself before even thinking of settling down. Now in her fifties, she's settled down in Half Moon Bay.

As we walk along the beach, I tell her about my concerns. I thought we could live apart and it would be fine, but it hasn't even been a week, and I already miss him.

I expect her to be disappointed. Instead, she tells me she's happy that I've found someone so good for me.

Even though I'm married, I'm still acting like I'm single, convinced that marriage can't work. Is it self-fulfilling? Am I the one with intimacy disorder?

My father and stepmother live in the suburbs, travel a lot, have their own lives. My mother and stepfather are involved in their community. My sisters, too, are married and settled down. Am I holding too tightly to the past? Is it preventing me from moving forward?

Shogo and I talk on the phone. We plan to see each other in the summer. I count the days until he flies to San Francisco.

I wish I could see him sooner. But it's a good sensation, that little ache.

It means I've let myself surrender that much more.

Helen Keller's Hand

Six months into our transcontinental marriage, Shogo comes to San Francisco, but it's not just for a visit. He quits his job, packs up his former life, and moves to America. And so we move in together, just like that. We rent a Victorian flat in Mill Valley, a wooded town across the Golden Gate Bridge. He applies for a Green Card.

We settle into California life. We work freelance, visit dog parks and bookstores, go to cafes and movies, hike the flanks of Mt. Tam. Shogo joins translation groups, puts out feelers for work. But he has trouble understanding spoken English in real time. The way English was taught when he was young was through reading, not speaking—and it was taught by Japanese, not native English speakers.

So each time I say a word he doesn't know, he asks me to spell it out. Then he promptly writes it out on his palm with his index finger. L and R pose a particular challenge. Words like *lyric* and *lovely* make him stumble.

I tease him about being like Helen Keller, but before long, he doesn't have to spell out the words on his hand. I find that I miss it.

But we're still newly-wet, and there are many cultural collisions. We find raccoons scavenging in our new basement. He calls them "rascals." They live up to that moniker, with their rambunctious mating sounds.

I make many mistakes in Japanese, too. When talking about politics, I say, "the wallet is going on strike." *Seifu* (government) and *saifu* (wallet) have only a vowel's difference. Since women control the household finances, Shogo is taken aback. Luckily for him, I realize my mistake.

To negotiate our respective languages, we set to work translating the poetry of Nobuo Ayukawa, an Imperial Army soldier in World War II who became a pacifist. Shogo's loved this poet since high school, and he was surprised I'd never heard of him. It's good to have this empty page in front of us on which to create something together.

We read each line aloud to each other, negotiate words and line breaks. Ayukawa's most famous poem, "America," about a country he visited only in his dreams, challenges us. Shogo's patience and diligence counterbalance my stubbornness and drive.

The poet borrows from Eliot, Mann, and others. The poetry is full of appropriations and is difficult to parse out.

> It was the fall of 1942.
> "Farewell! We will never meet again.
> And whether we live or die, our future is dark.

So, one by one, we disappeared from the town at night,
laughing at the way we carried our rifles
on our shoulders.
Old men with fake flowers on their chests
showered us with highest words of praise
as we headed for the killing fields.

I feel Ayukawa's spirit hovering over us as we work to translate his dispatches from the trenches. Shogo respects Ayukawa's struggle to keep the war memories alive, especially at a time when most people in Japan wanted to embrace "progress" and forget the past. Now, with America on the verge of another war, he feels a kind of imperative to bring this long-forgotten poetry to light.

After we finish the war-era poems, we set out to translate Ayukawa's later work, which depicts a man grappling with his country's growing material wealth and historical amnesia:

Fighting in the sordid world of profit and loss
your friends, good at mimicry, sing in chorus:
these are bad times.
They complain to a hostess in a lonely bar
that water doesn't turn into wine
that desire doesn't turn into more
consumption.

The poems written toward the end of the poet's life suggest he's arrived at a kind of peace with himself and his country:

The one who's able to forgive a little
is left with some leeway
to lighten their burden.

Though our outer circumstances are different from Ayu-kawa's, I can't help but wonder if there is something in both Shogo and my inner journey that might mirror his. There is a reason, I feel, that Shogo is drawn to this work. And that reason is why I am drawn to Shogo.

But the work is painstaking, and it's hard to squeeze it in between regular jobs. I suggest we apply for a grant from the NEA. Shogo thinks our chances are slim, that it's not worth the trouble. I apply anyway, filling out the application, refining the sample, and setting out stacks of copies on the kitchen table before mailing them out.

Then we begin another project. After reading *Memoirs of a Geisha*, we talk about empowered Japanese women, not those shuffling ten steps behind their men. The women I know, like Kyoko and Tomoko, are strong and independent, though they don't wear it on their kimono sleeves. Shogo and I decide to start writing a novel about a half-Japanese female ninja who comes into her powers to save her tribe. It's exciting to think of writing a novel together, trying to meld our cultures and voices to find common ground.

News comes; we get the grant! Encouraged, I prepare to submit the manuscript to Columbia University for a translation award. Now all we need is a publisher.

Maybe our luck will come in threes.

As we send the manuscript out, I'm amazed that we've finished this without killing each other in the process. Nothing in our relationship suggests that we would have, though, and this fear is clearly a throwback to past memories. More to let go of. We don't talk about children, about starting a family. Our books are our children, it seems, and I'm proud of this motley crew.

It's a Wrap

My maternal grandmother Molly comes to visit, stays with my mother in Sonoma.

Shogo's still shy about speaking in English, and it takes patience to understand him, patience many people don't seem to have. And of course, Grandma Molly doesn't know a word of Japanese, and her English comes out in a thick Yiddish accent, so I wonder how they'll communicate.

To be honest, I haven't always had an easy time connecting with this Russian-Jewish four-foot-ten dynamo, either. She usually keeps to herself, spending the first week in the kitchen and the next week on the couch watching soap operas. But by the time she leaves, my mother has hundreds of blintzes—cheese, blueberry, cherry, and strawberry—stockpiled in the freezer.

Molly brings her own blintz pan and takes over my mother's kitchen. After the formal introductions are out of the way, she rolls up her sleeves and gets to work. Shogo stands beside her, taking it all in. She has a system and a line-up, just like in a factory, but this observation seems to be breaking her stride. Since Shogo is just standing around watching, she puts him to work. He ties on an apron and washes his hands.

She shows him the ropes, step by step. If you think sushi chefs are particular, meet a blintz master. The crepes can't be too thin or too thick. You have to put just the right amount of filling in the center, then fold the crepe softly so it won't tear. Then there's the frying: The blintzes have to be lightly fried, but kept in the pan long enough to get a soft brown sheen. Not to mention the flip—a fork must be angled just right under the crepe to flip it over gracefully.

Even then, only one side is browned, because the other will

be fried after defrosting. It's a science, and Grandma Molly takes it very seriously. Shogo nods and takes it all in like a good *deshi*, disciple.

Even though Shogo can't understand Grandma Molly's Yiddish-laced English, and she can't understand his Japanese-accented English, they laugh and cook together in the kitchen for days.

I ask her what she thinks of him.

"I can't understand a word he says, but if you have a man who can cook, you should definitely keep him around," she laughs.

On the fourth day, the blintzes are done. Now it's Shogo's turn. He teaches her how to do the wrap, Japan-style, with a sushi-making lesson.

The rice has to be cooked just so, with exactly the right amount of vinegar, he explains. And you have to fan it to make sure it sticks together enough, but not too much. And when you put the *nori* in the bamboo roller, make sure to roll it tightly. Don't put too much filling in, or the roll will be lumpy and the nori will tear.

She's a good student, but says she won't be eating seaweed any time soon. She declares blintzes as the first culinary wrap, maybe even older than sushi.

I marvel as I watch them together. I'd assumed that Grandma Molly was the least likely of all of my family members to be able to relate to Shogo.

Wrong.

Before she leaves, Molly (octogenarian Jewish sushi master) and Shogo (young Japanese blintz master) cook a meal for me and my mother and stepfather. She makes sushi; he makes blintzes. It's a strange combination, but it works.

Then she gives Shogo his very own blintz pan. And because one good turn deserves another, he gives her a bamboo sushi maker.

She puts it in her suitcase to take home to Texas.

On her last night in California my mother Donna, her mother Molly, and I go to hear Adrienne Rich—the poet my mother read while our family was breaking apart, the poet I read a decade later trying to put myself together. Ms. Rich is older now, frail from arthritis, and walks with a lucite cane. We sit in the front row, inspired and enthralled to hear the words that have meant so much to us.

At the end of the talk, Ms. Rich asks us to stand up, acknowledges these "three generations of women" in the front row. I hadn't realized that she'd noticed us. I place my hands together at my heart and I bow to this woman who'd inspired us and so many others to come out the other side. And I see that we had. Somehow, we had.

Expatriate in My Own Skin, 1997

Shogo and I decide to try to buy a house. I take my English-teaching savings out of the bank and walk them down to Charles Schwab. I choose a fund that a friend's father had invested in. It's risky, but the funds are green, and he's made good money. When my small nest egg—hatched from my $500 life savings—triples, I count my blessings and close the account. Luck is on my side—it's just before a market crash. Kyoko has left Shogo a small inheritance, so we combine the funds and make an offer on a fixer-upper in a small village on the West Marin coast.

When the deal closes, we pack up Shogo's new blintz pan and move to a small coastal town at the beach, population two hundred. It's a bit "Wild, Wild West" with boozers, brawlers, and unannounced visits by the sheriff, looking for the prior owner, who's been charged with attempted vehicular manslaughter. But for the most part, the town is quiet and we can work.

We scrape by. We get hired to help on translations of a *Star Wars* documentary for the archives at nearby Lucasfilm, driving our beat-up car through rolling hills and farmlands. And once a week, Shogo drives several hours down the coast to Monterey to teach Japanese. We piece together a livelihood, and a life.

We adopt Aska, a rescued pit bull mix. We walk on the beach with her, which proves challenging because she's traumatized and has a tendency to fight with other females who look at her the "wrong way," which is just about every other bitch on the beach. But we work with her, patiently and steadily. We keep a short leash.

In this tiny coastal California town, with its lazy beach rhythms, where the lights go off at 8 p.m., my 24/7 Tokyo life starts to fade. But something tethers me to an even more distant past. I get asked to co-translate Japanese haiku that a Sacramento psychologist has found in her parents' attic after their death.

Her family had been interned in Tule Lake, California, during World War II, and she'd been born in the camp. Her father was eventually sent to a prison camp in North Dakota as a result of a series of difficult choices he'd made, thinking they would help his family. He'd sent his pants to his wife to launder, hiding letters and haiku in the waistband. The daughter had found a box with these letters, and had found my name in a translation group listing. My friend Hisako and I undertake the work, hoping to do justice to these searingly beautiful poems, written in what was surely this man's bleakest hour.

I also begin work on an anthology of wartime testimonials for the University of Hawaii's literary magazine, *Manoa*. Reading these testimonials of both victims and perpetrators, it is difficult to fathom the fact that "enemies" are now friends. But memories fade, and the generation that is passing on wants to make sure its history is not forgotten.

I'm not sure why work of this nature comes to me, but somehow, I've become a kind of bridge between cultures and languages, the dead and the living, worlds of war and peace.

Still, the work is intense, and sometimes nightmare-inducing. It makes me appreciate what I have—time, freedom, love. It also makes me question where I belong in the world.

One day I see a poster for a yoga class at a local dance center and do a double-take. Maybe yoga would be good for me, I think. I'd thought of yoga as something too "slow" and "old" for me, but this yoga is *vinyasa*, the brochure says—a moving sequence like dance. I decide to go.

The dance center is musty and wooden, the teacher is friendly and casual. She takes us through Sun Salutations, standing poses, backbends, deep stretches on the ground. I sweat and struggle, but when class is over, I feel light and happy.

That night, I sleep soundly.

And in the morning, when I sit down to work, I seem to be able to focus better.

I begin to practice yoga three times a week. The first few weeks I sweat buckets, and my thighs shake constantly in Warrior Two.

Then one day, the shaking stops—or rather, I stop caring about it—and I begin to discover fluidity in the movements. I feel sturdiness, strength, joy.

Then I meet the dreaded Camel Pose.

In Camel Pose, you're down on your knees, with your hands on your hips. You have to push your chest forward and open your heart. I have so much resistance to doing this, so much fear. I do the minimum, then sink back down into Child's Pose. Nothing escapes Jill, my teacher. She notices right away, approaches me gently.

"What are you afraid of?"

"I don't know," I say. All I know is that I want to come out of the pose. Now.

"Can you try to go there and breathe into it? Just be with what arises?" she says, one hand gently resting on my back, the other cupping my head.

Cradled in her hands, I explore the pose a bit more. My breast-bone feels tight, my breath constricted.

"Send the breath in," she urges.

And I do. I see how I've been folding into myself for so many years it's become habitual to hide my heart. I've developed an armor to shield myself from pain.

"If I take off my armor, I'll get hurt," I say.

"By holding it all in, you're hurting yourself more than anyone out there could be doing," she replies.

I don't want to investigate. Instead, I start to check out. But Jill stays on me, fierce and compassionate.

"Breathe," she says, staring intently into my eyes. "Don't leave. Go there."

I focus on my breath. With my chest lifted and exposed, I start to choke up.

"It's okay," she says steadily. "Go there. Go into it. Let the tears come."

I stay and breathe into the tightness, the holding, the contraction. I feel it softening, receiving the breath. The tears come. They keep coming. She wraps her arms around me, holds me as I cry.

I'm embarrassed, but she's not embarrassed. She's just there for me, staying with me, present.

After class, I feel exhausted, but also cleansed. So I keep going back.

I start to feel an inkling of possibility, a sense of the power of being open and free. I just have to breathe, slow and deep. And stay where I am.

Do not leave the room. Do not leave your body. Do not leave your heart, I tell myself.

Each time I get on the mat, I start to see, and break down, the walls I've built around myself. After my first few months of yoga, I get it: I'm an expatriate in my very own skin.

Practice

I fall in love with yoga as I fell in love with Shogo. Both seem the cure I've been waiting for my whole life. Or is it because I've opened my heart to Shogo that I've opened my heart to yoga?

I practice on the beach while Shogo does his karate.

I laugh to think that we were both smoking cigarettes when we met.

Stripped of my busy-ness, yoga helps me find space inside myself. I see that I've been running away from *me*. I've been hiding by throwing myself into work. I see the parts of myself I don't like. The parts that are impatient, selfish, lazy, demanding.

Jill encourages me to go deeper.

"Yoga is a self-healing practice," she says. "All you have to do is show up. It will take you where you need to go."

The yoga teaches me in a direct way that we all share feelings of insecurity, doubt, worthlessness. And that the more we connect to the shadow or hidden parts of ourselves, the bigger we become—the more we realize everything is connected. The yoga teaches me how to change myself, and to forgive myself and others. Actually it doesn't even have to teach me; it all seems to happen naturally through the practice.

Instead of trying to push away these feelings, I acknowledge them and let them be—and then they lose their power. I start to feel more peace, bliss, and connection. I start to approach a state of yoga—union.

I start to treat myself and my body better. I start to trust Shogo, and myself.

Stories

"Why do you hold yourself back?" Jill asks one day while I'm in Triangle Pose.

"What do you mean?" I feel I'm growing so much, not holding back at all.

"You're collapsing in the pose," she says. "Here, I'll show you."

She steps her feet apart, takes a deep breath, extends her arms, shifts her hips. She leans out over her front leg, places one hand down on the ground, then draws the other arm up into the air.

"Do you see it?"

I look at the pose. Her alignment is spot-on. Spine straight, fingers spread, with her gaze—*dristhi*—beyond her thumb, up to the ceiling.

"It looks perfect."

"Really? Look more closely."

I do.

She breathes. "Do you see any energy moving? Do I look alive?"

"I don't know," I say, suddenly doubtful. "Maybe not."

"Good," she says, deepening her breath. "Look down."

I look to where she is pressing the outer edges of her feet into the earth.

"Now look up."

I look up to where she reaches out through her fingertips, which radiate like the rays of a sun. She draws her arm behind her and opens her heart. Her whole body floods with energy. The entire pose lights up.

"Do you see the difference?" she asks between breaths.

"Yes!" I say, excited.

"The first was *doing* the pose. The second is *being* it," she says.

"I get it!"

"Now you try. Engage your muscles," she coaches me.

I nod, but as I take the pose, I feel frustrated, stiff. I see this action in her, but I don't know how to do it myself.

I come out of the pose. "I thought yoga was about surrender. Not pushing harder," I say. I'm loving the fact that my yoga practice is the one place I don't have to be ambitious, to push, to try so hard.

"I'm not talking about pushing. I just want you to awaken your potential."

I frown. Hadn't I done that back in high school with Mr. Sereno and the whole human potential thing?

She waves her hand away. "That was then, this is now. You're not the same person you were back then. You're not the same person you were last week, let alone twenty years ago," she laughs. "No one is. We need to keep growing."

"How?"

I get my answer when we practice kicking up into a handstand against the wall. Our legs scissor in the air like pinwheels. I keep trying to kick up, but fall down each time.

Other people kick up effortlessly. Some even balance in the middle of the room.

But try as I might, I can't.

I'm scared. It's fear that holds me back. What am I afraid of, falling or flying?

Jill has instructed us to hug into the midline, press up through our inner thighs and heels, and relax the shoulderblades. But as soon as I get partially upside down, I can't remember any of it and come crashing down again. So I try again.

Jill looks, but doesn't come up to me as I flail against the wall.

"Why aren't you helping me?" I finally ask, frustrated.

"I am," she says.

"How? How are you helping me?"

"By letting you work it out on your own. Just keep at it."

I try to kick up a few more times, but my arms won't hold my own weight. I land hard on the ground with an ungraceful thud.

"One day, you'll lift yourself up. It took me months to get it."

I want to believe her, but all I see is a wall in front of me.

"You keep thinking yoga is the pose, it's not. It's the process."

I nod. I know I've made this wall. And I know she's right, that I'm the one who's going to have to tear it down.

Finally, we come down to the ground, hug our knees into our chests.

"Carolyn Myss says that our biography becomes our biology," Jill says. "What this means is that events we haven't reconciled or forgiven are carried as debt on a cellular level. The body remembers. Ask yourself: what stories do you tell yourself about yourself?"

She speaks to us while we're resting in passive backbends, blocks under our sacrums.

I breathe into my heart.

"You might wonder how you move forward. You do that by showing up. By awareness. By being accountable," she says, circling the room.

"Accountable. What does that mean?" I ask from my mat.

"It means," she says, stopping to kneel down next to me and looking me straight in the eyes, "that you are not a victim. Even if hurtful things were done to you, you move on. You forgive. You don't have to forget, but you forgive. This is an empowered state. This is yoga."

After class, I sit with this question—the stories I tell about myself. The fact that I can actually see my life as a story feels significant. I realize that I'm tired of my story.

Lines from a poem arise, and I take out my notebook to write them down:

> She is tired of suffering.
> She is tired of telling her story.
> She's survived.
> Now she just wants to live.
> She knows that Midas died
> broken and weak.
> She knows you can't live on gold.
> All she wants to do is
> touch the sun.

The Attack, 1984

I go to the track at the Clark Kerr housing complex in Berkeley. I choose a weekend afternoon, when the track is peppered with a mix of young college students and grizzled veterans, most of whom probably ushered in the running boom of the 1970s.

The last time I came here, it was the School for the Deaf. Where no one could hear you scream.

It was the summer of 1984, and I'd just taken up jogging. I ran from my house to the track every morning. One morning, as I came past the corner of Belrose Avenue, a hand reached around my neck, pushed my shoulder, and knocked me down. I was dragged into the bushes. I stared up at a man with disheveled blond hair. He was wearing a dark blue T-shirt and red nylon jogging shorts that he was taking down. It happened so quickly.

I tried to lift my body from the ground, but I couldn't. It seemed to weigh ten thousand pounds. I was frozen.

I tried to scissor-kick my legs in the air. They didn't move.

Get up, I told myself. *Get up! You've got to get up!*

Nothing.

If you don't get up, he's going to rape you.

Then, in an instant, my mind split in two. I saw myself from above, sprawled out on the ground. I asked myself: *If you saw a girl lying on the ground, wouldn't you want to help her? Wouldn't you help her up to safety? Help her. Help her get up!*

I flailed, thrashed, wild as a Himalayan tiger. I screamed.

I pushed myself up, ran like crazy, ran all the way home. He hadn't harmed me. At least, not physically.

Later that night, I started to bleed. I thought it was my period, but the bleeding didn't stop. My boyfriend Jake drove me to the hospital.

"You were pregnant," the doctor said.

"Pregnant?"

"Yes, but you've miscarried."

After, Jake and I sat in silence in his car. Music from *Elton John's Greatest Hits* floated out from the eight-track player.

"I'm sorry this happened," he said.

"What part of it?"

"All of it."

"Someone Saved My Life Tonight" came on. I started to sing along. My version went:

I'm a butterfly. And butterflies are free to fly, so fly away. High away, bye-bye . . .

Jake laughed. "Where you gonna fly away to?" he asked, arm resting on the open car window, fingers dangling.

"Somewhere far away. I'm going far away."

"Right," he said. "Then what?"

"Then I don't know. I haven't thought that far."

He laughed louder.

I laughed, too, but I was determined.

Decades later, these memories resurface as I pass the clump of bushes. My feet pound the pavement. My heart pounds, too. My adrenaline is pumping, my body full of fear. But the past is not here anymore. Birds are chirping. People are smiling. The sun is shining.

There is no man in a dark blue T-shirt and red shorts.

And I am not on the ground, frozen.

I keep running and running and running. I run until the tears come down. But I am crying with gratitude. I thank Mr. Sereno for teaching me how to meditate. Was that why my mind split in two? If I hadn't had that awareness, would I have remained frozen? I think so. No. I know so.

The tears turn to laughter. I'm running and laughing like a maniac. Big belly laughs, crazywoman laughs. But it's Berkeley, so no one notices. And if they notice, they don't care.

I keep running.

I run until I feel.

I *feel*.

I *feel*.

And then I know that I can move on.

Lovingkindness

The next day in yoga, Jill teaches us the Lovingkindness (*Metta*) Meditation. She always seems to know exactly what I need. Is this a yogic power? If it is, I want it.

I sit on my mat, close my eyes, watch my breath.

I keep my spine long and my chest soft as I follow Jill's instructions. Step by step, I let myself be guided.

This meditation is designed to train your mind out of habitual negativity and ego. First, you send compassionate thoughts to yourself. Then you send them to someone with whom you have difficulties, then to someone you see often but don't know, then to the entire world. At first, it's difficult to send kindness to someone I feel has harmed me. Let myself get rolled over? It goes against everything I think I believe in.

But Jill seems happy. She believes in the power of this meditation, which she practices regularly. Are my beliefs incorrect?

I owe it to myself to give it a fair try.

So I hold an image of myself in my mind as I say the words:

> *May I be happy*
> *May I be free of suffering*
> *May I be at peace*

I hold an image of those who have harmed me as I sit and say:

> *May you be happy*
> *May you be free of suffering*
> *May you be at peace*

This is more of a challenge.

As I send them light and love, I know the harmful things

they've done come from their own unconsciousness, their own hurt and pain. I hold both of us in my mind as I sit and say:

> *May there be peace between us*
> *May the hearts of everyone be open to themselves and*
> *to one another*

Then I try to be limitless in my vision, holding the world and all its living beings in my mind as I say:

> *May all beings be happy and free of suffering*
> *May all beings be at peace.*

I do the Lovingkindness meditation for twenty-one days, until it becomes a habit. I start to feel more hopeful than I've ever felt before. Surprisingly, I don't feel small or weak sending compassion or kindness to my so-called enemies. I feel that it takes the edge off me, but in the best possible way. I'm not "looking for a fight" like I might have done in the past. I'm just being, and letting be.

And I dream, though still distantly, of having a family of my own.

A peaceful, loving family.

Sisters, 1999

Shogo and I go to Tokyo to visit his family, and I have a session with Dietmar, who asks where my son is. When we return, my sister Amy gets married. A few months later, she's pregnant. She invites me to the delivery to experience the joys of birth. This, she feels, will sway me to want to have a child of my own.

We've all envisioned her birth as a natural one, with harp music and massage and aromatherapy. When the day finally comes, though, it's what it is for most women—many hours of pushing, agonizing, enduring. The child refuses to come out.

Her ten-pound boy is packed so tight in her womb they have to use forceps to take him out during a C-Section. I've never seen the insides of someone's uterus before, let alone a baby being pried out of one. He's blue by the time they lift him out. But he's fine.

The doctor holds him in both hands. He's muscular and healthy.

"He looks like he is ready to move a piano," the doctor says, placing him in his father's arms.

When my sister comes to, she's mystified as to why her child is so big. Neither she nor her husband are big. After all, she reasons, she's a vegetarian and ate healthy food throughout the pregnancy, supplemented with daily protein shakes.

I raise my eyebrows.

"Protein shakes? Liquid protein? Wouldn't that go straight to the placenta?" I ask.

"Oh, don't be ridiculous," she laughs.

"Hello?" I say.

He's tested for diabetes. The test is, fortunately, negative.

It's pointless to quibble. Her child has been born; he's healthy, she's healthy, and all is well. He looks strong and powerful, like someone you'd want on your team.

I make a mental note about protein shakes. Just in case.

Ready

My middle sister Melanie has become a fashion designer, with her own shop and clothing line. She's also ready to be a mother. But her body isn't cooperating. She also has a metal plate screwed into her spine where her sacrum meets her lumbar. Due to years of high school gymnastics, her back is shot. She begins the adoption process.

A placement comes through. Melanie's baby is healthy and strong. She and her husband leave California and start a new life.

Shogo and I take a road trip to the Southwest to visit them, traveling the famous Route 66. We stop at the Trinity Site, where the atomic bomb was tested before being used on Japan. I'm surprised there's nothing more than a small roadside sign to mark the place. We pull over and look out over the sweeping sand dunes.

We stand there for a long time, thinking about those small detonations, and the larger ones that defined our two nations for generations. And when I think about the future, I think about having a family. The thought is so foreign it startles me. It makes me uncomfortable, and scared.

And that's a very good thing, I think. It means I'm getting somewhere.

If we ever have children, will our children and their grand-children believe that our countries were once mortal enemies?

Just like that, Shogo and I decide to try to start a family.

Tests, 2000

I pore over *Taking Charge of Your Fertility* like I pored over *Our Bodies, Ourselves* as a teenager. I follow all the advice. But six months go by, with no results.

Like many women of my generation, especially those from bro-ken families, I'd been ambivalent about starting a family for so long that when I woke up and realized I might want one, it was in fact, too late. My heart and mind are ready, but my body won't cooperate.

Making a baby had been something I imagined I'd do after I'd "gotten my shit together." And I thought, as many do: "If it's meant to be, it will be."

For so long, I didn't want to have a family of my own because I didn't want to bring a life into an untenable situation. If I wasn't happy and healed, how could I be a good parent?

Now I see that the muddy waters have helped me to grow stronger, more resilient. All the muck I've tried to wash off is really fertilizer to create a richer soil.

I dive deeper into my yoga. I sweep my arms overhead, open my heart, and salute the sun. I imagine bringing in light, joy, contentment. I breathe in inspiration and breathe out pain. Exhaling, I fold toward the earth, surrendering. Over and over again.

Still, it's often hard to get on the mat. Sometimes it's all I can do to take out a bolster and drape myself over it for Restorative Yoga, breathing into my pelvis.

Sometimes, that is enough. My pelvis needs some serious TLC.

I'm thirty-eight, so I go to the hospital for tests. I have a hysterosalpingogram, in which dye is put through a thin tube into the uterus and released. The dye should flow into the Fallopian tubes if there are no blockages. Of course, I have blockages.

I watch all of this through an X-ray beamed onto a screen in front of me. I see the dye passing through the uterus and Fallopian tube on my right side. But the left is another story. Unbeknownst to me, I have endometriosis, and scar tissue blocks the left tube. The technician suggests we try to shoot the dye into the tube again, so the force of the pressure might open it up.

It's incredibly painful, but we try it. I watch as the tissue dislodges a bit, opening up slightly. But not enough. We try again. The third time's the charm—the dye pushes through and opens the blocked tube. The pain is intense, but worth it.

I'm sure our child is around the corner.

I put on my samurai armor and buy some pregnancy test sticks.

Manipura

THIRD CHAKRA

From the Sanskrit term meaning "lustrous gem." The solar plexus
chakra, the third chakra, is located at the navel. It's the center of will,
manifestation. The element is fire.

When this chakra is balanced, you have healthy self-esteem, but
are non-dominating. You are in touch with your power and wield it
wisely. You have the power to heal yourself and others, are energetic,
spontaneous, and in control of your emotions. You are able to manifest
your dreams.

Anne Frank's Aunt

Shogo walks on the beach everyday with Aska. They cut quite a figure—a long-haired Asian man in a faded green Army jacket with a pit-bull/wolf mix chasing seagulls by his side.

Though Shogo is shy, and Aska sends the other dogs scampering away, he makes friends. One is a Swiss woman named Ruth, an artist who lives with her husband and teenaged son on the hill. Her husband does something with computers and travels a lot. He also speaks around ten languages. Shogo thinks he's a spy.

We meet for coffee or walks. Ruth grew up in a strict Catholic household. Her parents forbade her to pursue her art, so she ran away to Basel and worked at an antique store. The owner encouraged her to paint. I learn this one night at a party at her house. She tells me all this as she presents me with a gilded box, urging me to open it.

"I want you to have this," she says, holding the box out between us.

"Me?" I'm stunned. How can I receive a gift from this elegant woman, whom I hardly know?

"Go on, open it."

It's an antique silver necklace with hand-wrought filigree teardrops strung between beads of sparkling garnets. It's delicate, and very precious.

"I can't take this," I say.

"You must," she replies, broad smile dancing on her lips. "Turn around."

I do. She clasps it around my neck. The stones seem alive, their energy thrumming against my skin.

"So beautiful. It suits you," she says, sipping her white wine. "It's from the shop in Basel. It was owned by Anne Frank's aunt."

"Why me?"

"I've been waiting to give it to someone. When you're done with it, please pass it on to someone else."

"Are you sure?" I'm uncertain of what is expected, but aware that a complicated history is being played out. Like other Germans I've sometimes met over the years, Ruth seems to extend extra kindness to Jews—at least, to this one.

"It's so powerful. I don't know what to say. So . . . thank you."

She leans forward, kisses my forehead. Then she takes my hand.

"Let's dance." She draws me to the living room, where people are moving to the trance-like music waving scarves, whirling like dervishes, ecstatic. I reach for Shogo and pull him out to the dance floor, too.

If you're going to live in Northern California (in general) and West Marin (in particular), you might as well surrender.

* * *

Days turn into months, which turn into years. We hold out hope for a baby, but each month our hopes are crushed. We pour ourselves into our work. One day, good news comes unexpectedly.

We receive the translation award from Columbia University for our manuscript of Ayukawa's poems. So much time has gone by that I'd almost forgotten I'd sent in the application.

It's fitting that Ayukawa will finally get to come to the States because of his book, *America*. We're invited to New York for the awards ceremony at a campus library. My mother and stepfather aren't able to come, but Peggy and her husband will be in town and are able to attend. The last time I'd seen her was in Half Moon Bay, just after they'd bought land for their dream house. They'd hired a builder who'd fought alongside the Resistance in World War II. Peggy was happiest about that connection.

"I'm so proud of you," Peggy says. "I really believe we can do what we put our minds to."

"You helped me so much," I reply. "You were my lifesaver."

I hold Shogo's hand, happy we didn't give up, happy he didn't give up on me.

As we take the stage together, ten years in, somehow I'm amazed that this odd coupling has worked. Apart, we might have been solitary, pensive poets, mumbling our half-drunk rants into an open mike. Together, we took on projects we wouldn't have dared on our own. We'd been able to do what we loved, and somehow we'd survived.

"Let's keep going," I say as we leave the library and walk out into the New York night.

"*Ganbarimasu*," Shogo replies, using the Japanese word for persevere.

I'll do my best, he's saying.

I touch the garnet necklace at my throat. Somehow, I feel a kind of power that reaches back oceans and continents, years and worlds. I recall the frightened, embattled girl I used to be, knowing I'm no longer her.

Jill had once told me that we can learn our lessons with difficulty and pain, or we can learn them with joy.

The necklace reminds me: I always have a choice.

The Ring

After six years on the coast, Shogo and I move inland to Sonoma County to be closer to "civilization," or at least to a grocery store. Ruth and her family have moved, too, and we've lost touch. Their phone number isn't listed and email isn't their thing.

I keep hoping she'll come to the little yoga studio in Petaluma where I'm teaching. I go there to take a class from Nicholas and Amanda, young Ashtangis whose practice is full of light and love. One day in Nicholas's class, I surprise myself by kicking up into a handstand. Just like that, after months of flailing.

Just like that, I have the foundation. My fingers are spread, hands solid on the earth, negotiating the balance. My legs stay up in their air, as I draw my energy up from my core, radiate it out through my feet. It's almost effortless.

I can hold my own weight. And I feel that power Jill talked about. I feel the pose lit up from within.

I'm rooted to the earth. I'm held by the sky.

I'm grounded and I'm flying.

I'm free.

Nicholas comes by and tickles my toes.

I come out of the pose, rest in Child's Pose.

Something in me feels as if it's broken free.

Then we form a circle, practice laughter yoga. At first you fake the laugh, and before long, the laughter is real. You laugh from deep in your belly until your belly actually hurts.

Ha Ha Ha.

Ha Ha Ha.

The sounds stoke an inner fire, transform anger, feel empowering and freeing.

When I lay down to rest in Corpse Pose, I'm completely spent. Ready to let go. Released.

And I'm pulling away from the yoga studio parking lot when I hear someone call my name.

"Hey, Leza!"

I whirl around. It's Ruth, leaning out the window of her station wagon.

"I've been looking for you. It's so good to see you!"

She looks healthy and flushed. She didn't always look so—sometimes she was gaunt and pale.

She pulls her car up behind mine.

"What a coincidence!" we both say, smiling. Do either of us really believe in coincidence?

We get out of our cars and hug.

"I'm so glad I found you—I've got something for you," she says.

"Really? Not again!"

"Yes. Again. I've been hoping to bump into you," she says. Whatever it is can't wait. She fishes around in her car, and then comes back with a ring. Silver. Garnet. Old. It matches the choker. She holds it out, beckons. I take it, put it on. It fits.

"It's gorgeous," I say, overwhelmed.

"It's yours," she says. "It goes with the necklace. They have to stay together."

This time I don't argue. I put it on. This ring that had once been held by Anne Frank's aunt, who had once held Anne Frank's hand—a power stone if there ever was one—sparkles on my finger.

I see now that the stones are more than jewelry. They are amulets, symbolizing that we exist in a world where our ancestors by blood (relatives) and by spirit (heroes like Anne Frank) can come to us in a moment of need. This feels like something beyond coincidence. It feels like proof of interconnectedness—through time, space, and geography. Through life and death, war and peace.

It feels like grace.

HAIKU, HAWAII, 2001

Pele

I wear the ring and necklace on my first yoga retreat in Haiku, Hawaii. I go with my new teacher, Simone, and a group from Petaluma. Our inn is deep in the Maui rainforest. We practice yoga daily outdoors, eat healthy food, sleep deeply to the sounds of the jungle. I forget about my computer, my unfinished books, my unfinished life. The lush, tropical air purifies and cleanses me.

I sign up for a session of *watsu* massage, a combination of hydrotherapy and massage held in an outside tub. On the night of the session, the stars shine down upon us and the full moon hangs like a silver orb, bright in the sky.

It's billed as a rebirthing session, so I step into the pool naked.

"Is this how you want to do it?" Mara, the massage therapist asks. She's an incredibly statuesque Italian who looks, and speaks, like Sophia Lauren.

"Isn't everyone born naked?" I want to be reborn.

"It's up to you," she says, smiling.

"I didn't know we were supposed to wear a bathing suit."

"It's okay. Just lean back," she says.

She holds me in her arms. I surrender. She twirls me and twists me, and I let her hold my body, my head tilted back. I'm cradled in her arms like a baby.

I'm safe and comforted. I feel my body become light and weightless, free and fluid as she cradles me and swirls me into the watery womb.

Then she starts to sing to me, a lullaby in a language I do not understand. I do understand that some part of me is dying and being reborn, and her voice is so tender and beautiful, like a mother singing to a child. The rain showers down.

My body remembers when my mother held me as a tiny child. I let this holding be her holding. As I am held, I imagine my mother, too, is held and healed.

Tears stream down my face as Mara embraces me, and I let them. Can I let go in my life, like the way I am learning to let go into the yoga postures, into the possibilities?

Even though I'm still childless, I'm trying to see everything that happens to me as a window into possibility and magic.

I'm trying to see the small things, like getting *watsu* under a full moon in the rainforest or drinking tea under the stars at midnight, as miraculous.

And they start to feel that way. They start to *be* that way.

The next morning, after a steamy morning yoga practice, I sit down to meditate on the lanai, breathing in the wet, fresh air. The island spirits call to me through the hot, damp mists.

Out with the old, in with the new. I know that energy can't be created or destroyed, only transformed from one state to another.

After what might be three hours or three minutes, a voice echoes in my head.

It is very clear, and strong. I don't open my eyes.

"You must go to Tokyo and open a yoga studio."

I sit and breathe deeply. As if I hadn't heard it, the message is repeated.

I sit very still, wait for more messages. None come.

When the meditation feels finished, I open my eyes. No one is there.

Who spoke to me? Was it my own inner guidance? Was it the island's goddess, Pele, whose energy radiates from the powerful volcano nearby?

In the retreat's library, I open a book of local history and learn that Pele is the quintessential power woman—sometimes young and beautiful, sometimes an old crone. She has the power to destroy, the power to create. She's expelled from her homeland by a jealous sister, forced to wander. Finally, she settles on the largest volcano in the world, Mauna Loa. To this day, high above the sea, her sacred fires burn there. "Pele of the Sacred Land" is a goddess who devours land with her flames.

Is this why she wants me to leave my home and return to Japan, deep into the ring of fire? Do I really want to go from one fault-line to another, just when I'm finally feeling settled and at home in California?

I have no intention of returning to Tokyo, much less starting a business in a foreign country. I'm happy in California, happy in my quiet life. I dismiss the message. It's just too crazy to consider. . . .

BERKELEY

Out of Hiding

. . . Or so I think, until an invitation to my twentieth high school reunion arrives. I almost toss it, but then my childhood friend Helen decides to attend.

She's married, living in Los Angeles, teaching art history. She has no children, either. We commiserate, sometimes.

In the week before the reunion, more emails from old friends arrive, and we reminisce about Berkeley High. I understand how special it was—we had world-class jazz, drama, music, academic opportunities—amazing for a public school. There was an open gay and lesbian community and a variety of student groups and opportunities to connect with people from different classes, races, backgrounds. Some of us are lifelong friends. Why am I nervous about going?

Many of us are doing well, with families and partners, health, happiness, and successful careers. Others have not been as lucky. Some have committed suicide. Or died in fatal accidents. I wonder who will be there and what will happen when we show up.

Helen and I go to our friend Judith's before the party. I wear the necklace and matching ring from Ruth, as I do on special occasions.

We fix each other's dresses and make-up, like we'd done in high school. We're excited, and more than a bit nervous. We've managed to avoid all the other reunions, but the twentieth seems too big an opportunity to miss.

"If it gets weird, let's give each other the 'okay' sign and split," Judith suggests.

"How could it not get weird?" Helen says, laughing.

"Yeah, I agree. Let's see how long we can last," I say.

As we're getting ready to leave, Judith's brother Jon comes into the living room. He fixes his gaze on me.

"Don't mind him," Judith says, smiling sweetly and walking toward him.

"Why don't you go in the living room, Jon?" She prompts.

But instead, he comes closer to me and stares.

"It's okay," I say, though I am unnerved.

I remember how smart and strong Jon had been in high school. He'd been a star player on the basketball team, and was a straight-

A student. When he turned eighteen, he'd had a breakdown. He'd been institutionalized since then, but was at home on the weekends. It was a Saturday night.

"The war's over," Jon says, looking straight at me. "You can come out of hiding now."

"What?" I ask. I'm unsure if I've heard him correctly, but I have goosebumps.

"Sometimes my brother says strange things," Judith says, putting her arm around him and moving him toward the kitchen as she waves us toward the door.

"We should get ready to go," she says.

"Wait!" I say, turning back to Jon. "What do you mean?"

"I said the war's over, Anne. You don't have to hide anymore." His voice is steady and clear.

"The war is over?" I repeat.

He nods.

And did he really call me Anne?

"Thank you. I'm so happy to know that," I say. My hand goes instinctively to the necklace.

Jon smiles. He knows. He knows which war is over. He knows everything.

Later, I tell Judith about Ruth, about Anne Frank's aunt. I explain about the necklace and the ring. Judith listens, quietly. Then she reminds me that her parents were Dutch.

As the music blares, Judith explains how her mom had been in hiding in the Hague during the war as a teenager. She wasn't allowed to go to school and could only go out at night. A German Shepherd had kept her warm. When her family was killed, she'd gone to the States, alone, after the war. But she was never bitter—she was happy to be alive. Judith's father was Christian, and had gone to America in his twenties. There was little work in Holland, so the government was offering one-way tickets out. His family had helped the Resistance by delivering flour and sugar to families who were hiding Jews. She told me that her father's older sister, seventeen at the time, was out delivering supplies when she'd been caught by the Gestapo and was never seen again.

I'm rattled as we head into the party, with its disco lights flashing, but I think this has happened for a reason, that Jon has a message. I once read that schizophrenics can see things the rest of us can't. What did he see?

These thoughts swirl in my mind as Helen, Judith, and I talk to old classmates, dance, and reminisce. Then we get up on stage, joining the group of white, black, and Asian students for a group picture. Everyone smiles. Rufus is there and hugs me. I hug him back, wonder if he remembers harassing me, grabbing my ass.

He's now a politician—of course he is—with a big, happy family.

Almost twenty-five years after graduating, in the soft light of retrospect, Berkeley doesn't seem so harrowing. High school friends raising their children here claim it's the best place on the planet to live. Is it only me who wonders if it had really been so challenging? Had I exaggerated the difficulties? Judith says no. Helen agrees. We all went through the fire.

We take more pictures, dance some more, and laugh together. It's a special night.

When it's over, I know Jon is right: Part of me is still hiding, afraid of speaking my truth.

It's time to come out of hiding.

High Alert, 2001

One sunny day, two jets crash into the World Trade Center, and the twin towers come down. The country goes on a color-coded alert system. Red. Yellow. High Alert. Middle Alert. Low Alert. America goes to war with Afghanistan. Iraq is not far behind. In the aftermath of 9-11, nowhere feels safe.

When no evidence of weapons of mass destruction is uncovered, Shogo is out protesting in Petaluma, standing on the street corner with a handful of others. People throw rocks at them. If people are throwing rocks in Northern California, what's happening in the heartland? I don't even want to think about it.

Shogo goes on a solo trip to Tokyo. Solo, because I discover in the taxi to the airport that my passport has expired. Due to fears of terrorism, you can no longer get a fast renewal, so he makes the trip alone. When he returns a week later, he delivers some news.

"I want to go back to Tokyo," he says quietly as we sit down to dinner, our first together after his trip.

"What?"

Shogo explains. He's forty-three. He can still find work in Japan. But if too much time goes by, he won't be able to slip back into Japanese society again. After almost a decade in California, it's time.

"Do you really *want* to fit into Japanese society?"

"I want to have that option. I want to see if I can go back on my own terms."

I smile, remembering what happened when Shogo quit his job almost a decade ago. He'd been a journalist at a high-tech newspaper for twelve years. A few months after he moved to California, his coworkers called from Tokyo.

"What do they want? Are they asking for your advice?" I asked, surprised.

"No. They're thanking me."

"For what?"

"For quitting." He laughed, explaining that having been at the company for so long, he was the senior writer. But because he was stubborn and opinionated, and mainly because he had tried to organize a union, he would never get promoted. In Japan, where everything is done based on seniority, that meant no one who joined the company after him could get promoted, either.

So when he left, they could finally move up the ladder. That's why they thanked him.

Shogo's done his best here, but he feels he's come as far as he can. It's time to return.

I think about trying to talk him out of it, but it seems only fair that we move back to Japan. Besides, his father's getting older, and while we've been away in the paradise of Northern California for ten years, Hitomi has been doing their father's cooking and laundry. But Hitomi, now in her thirties, wants to start her own life—open her own business, move on. We can't ask her to take care of their father forever, can we?

It is Shogo's turn—our turn.

"What would I do there?" I ask.

Shogo takes this to mean I don't want to move. He gives me the choice in simple terms. I can stay in California, or I can go with him back to Japan.

I think it over. America is at war. The economy is not favorable to freelance translators, and much work is being outsourced cheaply. Our income has dropped. And, my husband is *chonan*. In Japan, *chonan* is a serious business. *Chonan* means the first-born son and heir to the family name and whatever fortune it may have acquired. It also means that the family is ultimately his responsibility, and that of the *yome*, the lady of the house.

Which, now that his mother is gone, would be me.

I pull out my *zafu* cushion, sit down to meditate. I breathe into my belly, softening my third chakra. I watch my breath. I drop beyond thought, if just for a moment.

When I come out of the meditation, things aren't really any clearer.

So I take out a piece of paper, write down the pros and cons of returning to Japan. I don't really want to go back to Tokyo, the busy life, the pollution, the stress. But I love my husband, and want to be with him. And I know that a good marriage is partly based on compromise—even sacrifice. The root of the word "sacrifice" is "sacred." In the highest sense, sacrifice is to do something completely for someone else, with no personal gain. As an independent American woman, that idea takes some getting used to.

What would I do in Tokyo? When I'd lived there before, I wrote, taught English, and worked as a copywriter. It was a good life for someone in her twenties. But California had made mush of me in the best possible way. I loved my slow pace, my friends, my yoga. I was also older.

What would I do in Tokyo now?

Then I remember Hawaii, the message I received about opening up a yoga studio.

"Do you think I can do it?" I ask Shogo.

"Anything's possible," he says.

I google "yoga studios in Tokyo." Only two come up. Maybe it's a good time to try. I tell my plan to the editor of a West Coast literary magazine whom I run into at a cafe.

"You're going to open up a yoga studio in Japan? Isn't that a bit like selling ice to the Eskimos or coals to Newcastle?" he says. The editor is known for his candor, and is famous for being cantankerous. I try not to take it personally. But I feel discouraged. Then I take a few breaths, step back.

So-called "Eskimos" have ice all around them, and their culture is built around it. It's so much part of the fabric of their life that they don't see it; but they need it more than anyone. And Newcastle? It once depended on its coal for survival.

Nothing is permanent. What if the ice disappears? What if the coal runs out?

Like the fish who can't see the water, the Japanese are surrounded by the spirit of calm, unity with nature, and an appreciation of the impermanent and imperfect. But somehow, in the rush to modernization and progress, many have forgotten it.

I decide to stay with Shogo, to go where he goes.

We pack our bags and get ready to move back to Japan.

As we're leaving, Amy gives me a box. It's full of baby clothes her son has outgrown.

"For your baby," she says, hugging me tightly.

I take a deep breath in, stack the box up with the others.

Later that week, I go to downtown Petaluma to a crystal shop. In the corner on a shelf is a little clay angel, designed to perch on a ledge. I buy it for the yoga studio I hope to open in Tokyo.

A few days later, we board the plane and watch the Pacific Ocean get smaller and smaller from the airplane window. Our dog Aska rides in the cargo hold below. I worry about how she'll adapt to Tokyo. But I know that being together is the most important thing for her, and for us. We're a family. She goes where we go.

It's not the first time I've made this crossing, and I have a feeling it's not going to be the last.

But this time, for the first time, I'm not making it alone.

·

Anahata

FOURTH CHAKRA

From the Sanskrit term for "unstruck," referring to the natural sound of the cosmos, a sound that is not made by "striking" an instrument, but instead one that is inherently present in all living things. The fourth chakra is the heart chakra, located at the heart center, the abode of the primordial sound (*shabda*). The element is air.

When this chakra is balanced, you are compassionate, kind, affectionate, able to forgive yourself and others, able to love and be loved. With self-acceptance comes the integration of opposites (male/female, mind/body, etc), the power of empathy, the ability of psychic healing. You are able to build harmonious relationships and are trusting. You experience a deep sense of peace and centeredness.

Heartlines, 2003

We move in with Shogo's father in Magome, once hilly pastures where the ruling shogun's horses were stabled. Due to its cheap rents, natural setting of woods, and proximity to downtown, Magome once attracted writers and painters. Nobel Laureate Yasunari Kawabata lived there in the 1920s. The "confessional" writer and "libertine" Chiyo Uno lived there in the 1930s. Later, Yukio Mishima had a huge Spanish-style mansion, famous for its parties.

My father-in-law, a literary critic known for writing about Japanese culture, had bought the house where Shogo grew up in the 1950s. It had been a bargain, and no wonder—it had once belonged to a politician who committed *hara-kiri* there when Japan aligned with Germany and Italy prior to World War II. The politician believed the alliance sullied Japan's purity.

I shudder when I go into that room. It reminds me of the haunted house of my childhood, only smaller and with *tatami* mats instead of a sarcophagus.

Surprisingly, just after we return, Shogo's father bequeaths us the house. We can move in and do as we like with it. (He'd bought a smaller lot next door in the 1970s, where he still had his book-lined atelier). Because the place is falling apart, and because I'd always felt strange when I walked into the room where the politician took his life, we decide to tear the old house down and build a new one. We use the money from the sale of our California fixer-upper.

We meet with the architect, draw up plans for our new

house—a duplex to be shared with Hitomi and Shogo's father. His atelier and bathroom will remain separate, but he'll share a downstairs kitchen and bath with Hitomi. Her bedroom will be upstairs, adjacent to our house. When drawing up these complicated plans, which have to accomodate everyone, we discuss whether or not to build a child's room. There's simply no place to put an empty room—we cannot justify having one when space is at such a premium. I give in, with a heavy heart.

And then I get busy, as there are gifts to be given. In Japan, there are always gifts to be given for appreciation, for apology, for "social lubrication." All in the spirit of harmony, or *wa*.

In the West, building your home is an individual affair. You make the plans, get the permits, and start construction. In Japan, everyone has to be consulted, from the neighbors to the earth gods.

Shogo sends me to a department store to buy gifts for the neighbors. Those at the perimeter will receive towels. Those closest will get gourmet boxed cookies. We go from house to house, apologizing for the impending disturbance as we offer the gifts. The neighbors take them with both hands, and bow.

When the time comes, the old house is torn down and hauled away, board by board. Then, it's time to request formal permission from the earth gods to rebuild.

Though Shogo's father is not religious, he summons a Shinto priest to perform a ground-breaking ceremony. The earth gods—*kami*—have to be appeased. The priest arrives, resplendent in ornate headgear and traditional silk ceremonial garb—right down to his stark white *tabi* socks.

He purifies the space by putting small branches of bamboo on each corner, adorning them with white streamers, and connecting them with sacred rope. He places a small evergreen branch on a wooden altar, symbolizing the physical manifestation of the *kami*. The priest then addresses the gods, offering gratitude and respect. He incants prayers for smooth construction—the *kami* will be disturbed by bulldozers and other heavy equipment, so we ask them to forgive us our trespass.

He brings out a wooden scythe, pick, and shovel to pacify the earth. My father-in-law approaches a small mound of dirt, uses the scythe to cut a symbolic tuft of grass stuck in its top. The construction company owner strikes the ground with the pick. A worker digs into the mound with the shovel. Shogo and I get to dig, too, heaving shovels of earth over the pit.

Then we raise a glass of ceremonial sake and toast the *kami*. With their blessings, harmony will prevail.

It is not lost on me that a Japanese man and his Jewish American wife are building their own "house of dreams" where a man once took his life because his country had allied with an Axis power in a time of war.

Four months later, we move. The *kami* have been on our side—construction has gone smoothly and quickly. We set up an indoor altar made of cedar, to make offerings of thanks to the household gods. It hangs at the entryway.

I place a camellia flower in an antique blue-and-white vase on the altar. It was Shogo's mother's, and the flower is from a tree she planted decades ago. I feel her spirit there.

But something is missing.

I stand back and look. The entryway doesn't feel right.

A week later, we get a package in the mail. My mother has sent a *mezuzah*.

Like the one from our house in San Francisco, the house that almost burned down.

We hang it on the wall and say a blessing: *May the divine spirit fill this house—the spirit of love and kindness and consideration for all people.*

On the left side of our entryway is the Japanese altar.

On the right is the Jewish *mezuzah.*

And in the middle, there is the door.

Unexplained

As we settle into our cultural push-pull, we move ahead with starting a family. But my body refuses to cooperate.

When a macrobiotic diet doesn't work, I eat pork, as a Chinese medicine doctor suggests. And sometimes I eat red meat, as some Western doctors suggest, to build up the iron in my body. I brew and drink a concoction of bitter Chinese herbs morning, noon, and night.

I try everything my maternal friends recommend, everything that has worked for them, or someone they know, or someone who knows someone they know. This includes evening primrose oil, wheatgrass, lymph drainage, abdominal massage, psychic healing, a thousand different vitamins and supplements, and even prayer.

I don't know whom I'm praying to, exactly, but it makes me feel better to try everything. And when I get very quiet, I hear a child's voice calling me.

"Don't give up," it says. "I'm out here."

And so I persevere. *Ganbarimasu.*

Nothing works.

Finally, I go back to the hospital. But the Western doctors can find nothing wrong with me, other than my age. I'm just another case of "unexplained infertility."

I call Peggy. She tells me not to give up. But just in case, she tells me to start thinking about Plan B.

The problem is, I don't have one.

Shogo says, "*Nana korobi ya oki*—fall down seven times, get up eight."

I take refuge in my marriage, and refuge on my yoga mat. And I find myself down on my knees in Child's Pose often.

It helps me to soften, to surrender, to ground myself. I imagine an umbilical cord stretching from my belly all the way down through the floor, cutting straight through the crust of the earth, connected to the core of the Great Mother Gaia. I breathe in and she sustains me with her energy. I breathe out and I give my gratitude to her.

I soften the back of the heart, my "wings." I breathe and I keep my head low to the ground, listening, even though I feel my wings are somehow clipped.

Unlike the huge, raucous crows that make their home in our garden. They steal our broom thistles to make nests for their young, sweep down in territorial wars. They've come down from the countryside, where their mountain tree-homes have been torn down.

They caw late at night and early in the morning, restless, liminal. The neighbors complain. The crows can be dangerous, the nest should be removed, they say. But I don't want to evict them. They belong here as much as we do, I think. Though they're not particularly welcome in the city, Tokyo has become their home.

I see in these crows a mirror for myself. Will I ever be at home here, or anywhere?

Am I at home within myself?

Mr. Sereno's words from so long ago return: "You can't walk out the door. You stay—and then you experience yourself just as you are. Not the story, not the ego, but what's behind the story. The space of unity, of wholeness. Of love," he had said.

Over and over again, I go back to my breath, my yoga. I return to my body.

I go outside to the garden—that wild overgrown place where Shogo's mother planted her dreams. I feel the sun on my skin, the warmth in my body, the hum of primitive nature around me, even in this thoroughly modern city. I understand that yoga has little to do with the poses, or even the breath. It has everything to do with owning yourself—from the grossest layer right down to the most subtle energy. Owning your body, your thoughts, your speech, your actions. Owning *my* body, myself. Being *embodied*.

I look up at the various trees Kyoko planted. And there it is—a pomegranate tree.

I understand that my place is with Shogo.

He is my *beshert*. My destiny.

Where I stay.

Sangha

I move forward with plans to open a yoga studio. Starting a business in a foreign country is daunting, but I try not to think about all the things I can't do. I remember the voice from Haiku, Hawaii, and I keep moving, one step at a time. The benefits I've gotten from yoga are so great I want to share them. That desire motivates me to keep pushing on to make it happen.

Besides which, when we decided to move back to Tokyo, I ordered thirty yoga bolsters, fifty blankets, and twenty five-pound sandbags from a supplier in San Francisco. I also ordered thirty silk neck pillows and thirty lavender-filled eye bags. They'll be coming soon, and I don't have anywhere to put them. I need to rent a place, and soon.

Having lived in busy Tokyo before, I know I want to share Restorative Yoga, a deeply relaxing practice that almost anyone can do. You lie back on bolsters, blankets, and props and let them open you up. You relax and let go. It's like a slumber party.

Soon, we find a small place in the center, close to the main train line. It's in an old building and opens to empty space and light. It's quiet, set back from the street, and affordable. It's been on the market for a year because the owner refuses to take out a large credenza. But the storage space that's a deal-breaker for everyone else is perfect for me—it's a great place to store the yoga props winging their way over.

In California, we'd been living surrounded by the sea and the mountains and open space and green. In Tokyo, there's really not much green outside of a cup of tea. I want to make the studio green and calm and feminine, with a round moon-window shape. I want to create a little oasis where people can discover and be their authentic selves through yoga and meditation.

An architect friend takes some bamboo from Shogo's dad's garden and brings it into the space for accents. In this way, we bring Kyoko's teahouse inside.

When the remodel is done, I'm ready to open. But the props are held up at customs. The inspectors have never seen such things and have to check every bolster, sandbag, and eye pillow for drugs.

Finally, we get the green light. When the yoga props finally arrive, they fit into the credenza perfectly.

I unwrap the angel statue I bought in Petaluma. It goes on a perch overlooking the studio. If the angel ever falls, I tell myself, it's time to move. I glue it down, just to be sure.

I name the studio Sun and Moon Yoga, after the yin and yang

of life, after the complement of "sun" and "moon" side channels into the central channel, where contentment abides.

I wait for the students to arrive.

No one comes. I try not to panic, to trust that voice I'd heard in Hawaii. After all, it was in Haiku that I'd heard it. Japan is the birthplace of haiku. The gods have to be happy, right?

I contact old writer friends, hoping they'll show up and give yoga a try. But they're busy with deadlines, and their socializing is largely done with cigarettes and booze, two habits I'd given up when I'd taken up yoga. If I hadn't, an alcohol daze would have been my refuge. I had been going down that road fast. So fast that when I'd introduced myself to a Japanese woman at an art opening a decade ago, she told me, "I've met you many times before. You never remember because you're always drinking." Japanese people are not generally known for criticism or bluntness, so it must have been really worthy of comment. Shortly after that, I decided to get sober.

Now, light streams in through the windows. I try to stay in the light, to keep practicing and trusting, letting myself embody the space with my own practice, my breath.

If you build it . . .

This is my mantra.

I sit and find silence and stillness, welcoming those qualities in the space by myself.

I hope and I pray.

Finally, one woman comes, a lawyer who says she's been wanting to practice yoga for years. Catherine's my only student for weeks. We have a blast together. She even kicks me in the face one day and chips my front tooth. I'd been standing over her, explaining how to get into Forearm Stand when she decided to just kick up into the pose.

We laugh about it later, after the swelling subsides. And I learn to stand to the side.

Slowly, more students arrive, bringing their friends. And their coworkers. And their friends' coworkers. They sweat out their stress and pain.

"I realize I've been holding my breath my whole life," they say. I know what they mean.

They do partner yoga with people they've never spoken to, touch people they've never seen before. I offer economical community classes for charity, even though people tell me it will never fly in Japan, where brands and luxury goods signify value and inexpensive means unworthy.

I don't listen. It flies.

In a city of millions, we do something revolutionary. We make friends with strangers. We make friends with ourselves. We make a kind of peace in a city of chaos. We find silence in a world of noise.

Before we know it, we have a *sangha*, a community.

And I finally have a home.

Lost in Translation

Two months after I open the studio, I get a phone call from Nihon Television. They want to know if I'd like to teach Restorative Yoga to Takashi Okamura, star of the Japanese comedy show 99 *Size*. I don't have a TV, so I don't know who Okamura is. But teaching yoga to a comedian sounds like fun, so I say yes.

The next week a crew of young Japanese guys comes to set up the scene. We get out the bolsters, pillows, sandbags, belts, and blankets. The room looks like a sleepover party.

"Is this yoga?" the star asks. He's small, compact, wiry, a meteorite of energy.

He mixes rapid-fire jokes with kabuki-like facial expressions and wacky body language, like Kung Fu Panda and the actor Toshiro Mifune on speed. I set him up in the yoga poses.

They've made Japanese cue cards for me, but the cards are in English romanization so I can read them. The romanization is a mess, and I can't make out the words. But the cameras are rolling, so there's no time to ask questions. The assistant flips the cards.

Kimochi ii deshoo (It feels good, doesn't it?) is written, incorrectly, as *Kimochi ii derou*.

The words flash before me, and I panic. I'm not sure if I should read what is written or say the phrases correctly. I decide to read what is written.

"*Kimochi ii derou*," I say, drawing the strange words out just as they are written.

Okamura's face contorts into a clownlike expression of puzzlement, and he bursts out laughing as he repeats the offending phrase.

He does a little dance. I do a little dance.

The writers furiously write more cue cards, each time making them more deliberately strange and twisted. We're on a roll, improvising together. I just go with it.

Sara Shivani, a yogini and actress who is fluent in Japanese, does some partner yoga with Okamura, and has a blast.

We're rolling around on the floor, laughing like hyenas.

Later, the TV station brings some props into their studio and devotes an entire program to Restorative Yoga.

From that point on, the studio is full.

Apparently, there was nothing like being on Japanese TV and playing a hapless *gaijin* to pique the interest.

People begin to recognize me on the street, stop me in elevators. "Aren't you that yoga lady?" they ask.

This means I can't eat as I walk down the street, another of my bad habits. (In Japan, eating in public, especially while walking or on the train, is considered the height of vulgarity.)

The students tell me they enjoyed the show, that they'd never seen a yoga teacher who laughed and didn't take themselves so seriously. At that time, most yoga teachers in Japan taught from an elevated platform at the front of the room and never came down.

Japan's teaching me how to laugh at myself, and while the yoga studio gives me a safe place to surrender, in private I'm still suffering. I need to keep letting go.

Proud Flesh

I go for my weekly massage to try to hammer away at the stiffness in my shoulders.

"What are you protecting yourself from?" the massage therapist asks, not unkindly.

I sigh, wondering how much to explain. It feels like such an old story, but the fact that it still triggers something in me means that I've not quite let it go.

"When I was younger, I was around a lot of violence," I say to the masseuse, not wanting to get into my "story."

"It's time to deal with the pain," the masseuse says. "You keep waiting for it all to magically go away, but it's just getting more entrenched."

"How do I deal with it?" I ask. "I've been trying."

"That's your journey," he says. "Ask your heart to tell you."

I stare down at my heart. In my eyes, it's covered in blood and slime.

I want to be happy. I want to feel that I deserve to be happy. Why is that so hard?

In her book *Fierce Medicine*, Ana Forrest writes of a horse she tended when she was young, a gelding with distemper. A lump at his throat cut off his breath. It needed to be lanced so he could breathe. His wound developed something called "proud flesh," thick scar tissue that needed to be cleaned and broken down so that healthy tissue could grow again.

Ana cleaned the proud flesh, peeled away at the dead scabs, and tended to the horse's wound so that the diseased tissue could fall away, and true healing could begin.

Humans also develop proud flesh around our wounds, and it's often too painful to cut away so that we can start to heal.

I start to visit an acupuncturist, a raspy-voiced woman who sticks hundreds of dagger-like needles into every part of my body, even into my womb.

I feel like a porcupine. I flinch each time the needles go in. They're Chinese-style, thick needles, not thin Japanese ones. Every time I cough, my innards are punctured. She massages me with hot olive oil before putting the needles in, and that helps, but only slightly.

The clinic's building is old, and it shakes each time the nearby train passes. It smells of moxibustion; thick clouds of smoke hang in the air. I hear snoring from the curtain beside me. A famous Japanese athlete is getting fertility treatments as well.

This acupuncturist is also a brain surgeon, literally. At night, a helicopter comes and takes her to another hospital, where she practices Western medicine. She takes care of twenty-two cats. She doesn't sleep. She says she doesn't want children of her own but wants to help women who desire children have them. She knits booties for her clients. Blue for those who have boys, pink for the girls. She also bakes them cakes.

I'm impressed by her stamina and generosity. She covers my body with hot towels to get me to soften. She spreads olive oil on my shoulders, massages the tight muscles. Then she starts to put the needles in, followed by moxibustion.

It's hard to relax. I begin to see my acupuncture as an endurance test. If I can let go during this, I can let go during anything. I can get pregnant. *I can*, I tell myself like a mantra, imagining a little baby growing within my body underneath the needles.

I do Qigong sessions, where I feel my womb being turned upside down and inside out like a washing machine. I feel the energy of every man I've ever made love to being released from deep within me. Except for one—Jake—the Swedish artist who wanted to have an "open relationship" and got me pregnant, that first and only time before the attack at the School for the Deaf. I'd lost the pregnancy, but that energy seems to be lingering.

I try to release it, too.

In meditation, I notice the thoughts and desires coming and going, and I notice myself noticing them. In this way, I can distance myself from them.

"*Neti, Neti, Neti,*" I say. *Not this, not this, not this.*

Circling around my thoughts and my awareness of my thoughts, I sometimes forget that I have a body as well—forget the aches and pains, the clicks and clacks of impending middle age.

Sometimes I'm able to dwell for longer periods in the space between my thoughts. This spaciousness is delicious, calm, curative.

And sometimes, I still hear the voice of a child in my head.

"Don't give up," it says. "You will find me."

Is it the soul of a child calling to me, or my own inner child, asking to be heard?

Does it matter? If it's a child, I think, he's a bit of a trickster.

"When you get here, I'm going to read you the riot act for making me work so hard!" I say.

I swear I hear him laughing.

Baby Bump Watch, 2005

I try to remain optimistic. But my optimism wanes each time another friend gets pregnant, or I open the newspaper and see another celebrity with child. Shouldn't it increase to know that Angelina Jolie, Britney Spears, Gwyneth Paltrow, Gwen Stefani, Jennifer Gardner, Jennifer Lopez, Julia Roberts, and Halle Berry have become mothers—even "oldies" like Brooke Shields and Marcia Cross?

Then a fifty-six-year-old woman delivers a baby. It's all over the news, and I never hear the end of it.

"See? It's never too late," people say helpfully.

"We don't know the details," I respond. Was it even her egg? Did she do IVF? There are many paths to pregnancy, I now know, and many are far from straight.

I google "pregnancy after 40." I want to know what the odds are. The real odds. The celebrities make it look so easy. Maybe they've all used donor eggs.

I commiserate with Melissa, a hard-core Ashtanga yogi with a vigorous yoga practice. She's been going to the same acupuncturist as me for half a year now. She's decided to interrupt her treatment and go to Mysore to study with her *guru*, and then to Chicago.

Back in Tokyo, Melissa tells me she is pregnant. She tells me about her herbalist in Chicago, who has given her a suitcase of herbs that she believes have helped her to achieve, and are now helping her to sustain, her pregnancy. I email the herbalist. She emails me back, suggesting I do IVF. What kind of herbalist recommends IVF?

I call up Melissa.

"I don't want her to tell me to do IVF! I want her to help me balance myself."

"You're balanced. Come on! It's a baby you want. IVF gets results."

"I just don't want to give up. I want to heal from within," I say.

"Who says you're giving up? Do IVF and *then* heal," she says, ever the tough Chicagoan.

She invites me to have lunch with her, but I can't. I tell her the truth, that I can't face her pregnant belly. She writes me back and thanks me for my honesty, says she's sorry that I'm in "so much pain."

We don't see each other for months, and emails drop off. Then she writes, saying she wants to come to Mysore-style class at the studio. She's eight months pregnant.

I tell her I don't think that's such a good idea.

She says, "I know my body, what not to do."

"That may be true," I say, but I don't feel so sure. And as a studio owner, ultimately it's my responsiblity if something should happen. She's forty-one and eight months pregnant with her first child after a miscarriage. Why does she need to do such vigorous yoga? Can't she just wait until after she delivers? If something happened, I'd feel horrible.

So I say no.

And she stops speaking to me.

Shortly after that, I find out she's been ordered to go on bed rest. I don't know if she'd been practicing yoga elsewhere or not. Her baby is born healthy by C-section. She's fine.

I'm relieved, but also a bit upset to have been put in such a position. I get out my mat and practice backbending. I move into the dreaded Camel Pose, which is not so dreaded anymore.

I breathe into my heart, softening and releasing. I keep opening, and when I feel like my heart will break, I stay a bit longer and breathe some more. *Let go. Let go*, I tell myself.

I put more energy and effort into the yoga studio, creating workshops, teacher trainings.

More and more women come, wanting to get pregnant.

I teach them Restorative Yoga, help them breathe into their wombs, create space, soften their hearts and minds.

Many of them get pregnant, have babies.

They ask if I'll be their baby's godmother, and I say yes.

I hope that if it can work for them, maybe one day it can work for me, too.

Elegy

I meet my friend Ted, another American yoga teacher and writer living in Japan.

He has a painful story, which yoga is helping him heal.

He took his three-year-old boy up to the mountains in Tottori, Japan. The boy ran ahead, as little boys will do. There was a wooden footbridge. It hung over a steep ravine, a hundred-foot drop. The boy ran onto the footbridge. The footbridge was made of planks of old wood. Not many people walked in the mountains anymore. There were gaps in the planks. Big gaps.

Ted watched.

Every year on the day the boy died, he posts a memorial picture of his son on his blog. The boy playing a drum set. Standing in front of a samurai helmet. Smiling for the camera. Making the peace sign with both hands. No words, no commentary. Only his son's picture and the word "elegy."

To remember. To honor.

Life is not safe. I know that. Nothing is certain. Things we hope for, dream about, come or don't come, and then are gone.

I meet with Ted whenever we can. In our own ways, we both mourn our lost children.

Somehow, we've been drawn together in this strange world to mirror each other's pain. To give each other comfort and hope. *We will move on*, our mutual presence seems to say. We give each other that.

I wonder how he must feel when he sees happy families.

Everywhere I turn, I see pregnant women—mothers pushing strollers, shopping, talking absent-mindedly on their cell phones as their kids throw tantrums.

What I wouldn't give for a screaming child, I think. I try not to wallow or judge, but I fail. I wonder why or how they've been able to give birth to a child and I have not. *Don't be a victim*, I say to myself.

And I try, I really try.

I know that if I begrudge these mothers their happiness, or even their frustrations, I'm operating from a sense of scarcity, a poverty consciousness that says there is a limited number of children to go around—not enough for me to have mine.

I try to smile, be happy for their happiness.

The mothers don't notice me, of course. And my act is not for them. It's for me, to change my way of thinking, to move beyond comparison.

As the months turn into a year, and no child is conceived, I take heart from the words of Anne Lamott, who's written that you don't need to have children to be complete. Plenty of selfish people have children, while many "evolved" people choose not to.

The same chances of awakening and connection exist for both "breeders" and non, she states. Of course, this doesn't factor in the possibility that some people don't *choose* to be childless, but the thought soothes me nonetheless.

Shogo and I talk about our disappointment.

He says I shouldn't feel badly or blame myself. He says it's okay, that we have each other. We can adopt more dogs, sponsor a child, spend more time with our nephew, and find other ways to become parents.

A psychic friend who sees a picture of Shogo and me in a newspaper when our new book comes out says she "sees" our children with us.

I want to see what she sees.

I sit and meditate. The image of a child just won't go away.

I am *sure* that Shogo and I can create a family.

I just have to change my picture of what it means to create.

I reframe the desire in my mind. It's not so much that I want *to have a child* as to experience *being a mother*.

How can I be a mother right here, right now?

I need more open space around me. I need to make room in my womb.

It's hard not to feel disillusioned. It's gotten too hard to handle all the hope and disappointment. The feeling like we're coming so close, yet staying so far away.

It feels like a gambling addiction. *Maybe I'll get lucky. Just this once*, I think.

So I try again. And fail again.

Shogo has stuck by me, supported me, nurtured me, taken care of me, gone to the hospital with me, held my hand as the acupuncturist twisted those thick needles into me, fixed me herbs, given me treatments, interpreted for me, never complained.

I know he's done his best and so have I.

"Maybe it's time to give up," Shogo says one day.

A friend sends me this haiku by Ikkyu:

> Wife, daughters, friends—
> this is for you.
> Enlightenment is one failure after another.

If enlightenment is one failure after another, I'm surely on my way.

Vishuddha

FIFTH CHAKRA

From the Sanskrit term for "pure" or "purification." The fifth chakra is located at the throat and is known as the throat chakra. The element is ether.

The fifth chakra is considered the center of communication, self-expression, poetry, speaking truth, and inner listening. When this chakra is balanced, you have mastered self-expression, have good communication skills, are creative and inspiring, and have relationships based on mutual communication, honesty, and respect.

Amma, August 2005

All the effort, pain, and disappointment of chasing motherhood has become too much to bear. I start to wonder if I've made a mistake by coming back to Japan. I can't seem to find the half-full glass.

Tokyo is my nemesis—the city has changed since I last lived here. There are more cars, more cell phones, fewer smiles. And unlike California, there's little organic food available, and when it is, the prices are outrageous. People smoke everywhere, on the street, in cafes. I know I shouldn't be a hypocrite, I used to be one of them.

But still.

"Where's your yoga?" Shogo asks when I run down my litany of complaints about the city.

He's right. I've forgotten my breath. And I've forgotten that I chose to come back here for Shogo, who gave up everything and went to America for me.

I consider going on a pilgrimage to the yogic motherland —India.

"What do you think?" I ask Shogo.

"Go," Shogo says. "When we have a child, you won't be able to go, so now's the time."

I hang on that one little word—when. Not *if*, but *when*.

So I sign up for a teacher training with Shiva Rea at an Ayurvedic center in Kerala, southern India, and I pack my bags.

Like many Western yoginis, I've wanted to take a pilgrimage to the motherland for years, but when I had the time, I didn't have the money. When I finally had the money, I didn't have the time. Now, by a stroke of good fortune, I have both.

I hand over Sun and Moon to the care of a British angel named Em, who will keep things running smoothly in my absence. I know it's in good hands, and that frees me to fly. I head out to India, hoping it will be the perfect place to heal and to find the mother within.

Arriving at Trivandrum Airport after midnight, I take a waiting taxi to a retreat by the ocean. I arrive after midnight and sleep in a grass hut. Crows caw, like they do in Tokyo. But wild dogs howl throughout the night, sending me into a hallucinogenic state before I drift off. The sound of the waves wakes me in the morning. A buffet breakfast of curries and yogurt and freshly squeezed juices awaits.

Shiva is a force of nature—yogini, writer, dancer, healer, businesswoman, mother. She supports musicians, is an environmental activist, is engaged. She teaches pranic *vinyasa* flow, moving with the elements, embracing the sacred pulse in everything. From Shiva we also learn *kalaripayattu*, a kind of southern Indian capoeira. We move in the heat, sweat shimmering, dripping, joyous, and free. Shiva's friend Sivkumar plays live sitar to accompany our classes. The beauty of it all makes me weep.

On a free day, fellow travelers—singer Daphne Tse and yoga teachers Coral and Kelley—and I hire a jeep to take us to an ashram in Kollam. After breakfast, a driver takes us along potholed roads, skirting the palm-fringed backwaters—rivers, canals, and lagoons that run inland and bustle with boats ferrying fruit, fish, and cargo up the coast.

Our Jeep shares the road with cows, farmers, women carrying loaded head-baskets, motorcycles overflowing with families. When we hit giant potholes, my head hits the ceiling. The cacophony outside is matched by the Bollywood hits blaring from the speakers inside the Jeep. It's a crooked road, with lots of obstacles. As within, so without.

Hours later, we arrive at an iron gate in front of the massive pink concrete ashram. In the auditorium where Amma, as she is called, is giving blessings, thousands of people sit on the floor, chanting devotional songs, meditating, or sleeping while they wait for their blessing. I feel peaceful and hopeful.

It's an auspicious day. Amma, a soft, grandmotherly woman in her late fifties with thick brown hair threaded with gray, is dressed like Devi, the female aspect of the Divine. Wearing a gilded silver headdress and flowing blue-and-red robes, she sits on a podium surrounded by devotees. For hours, she opens her arms to hug people, not stopping even to go to the bathroom. I'm struck by how emotional many are. Some hold on to her and have to be pried off. Many weep and wail.

Is it her pure heart they're so taken by? It's believed that the energy transmission received in the presence of a holy one awakens those same qualities in us. Amma teaches, "One is not the limited body and mind but eternal blissful consciousness." Are all these people tapping into this blissful consciousness? Can I?

We sit in Amma's direct line of energy, melting into a calm spaciousness. Though she is not a biological mother, Amma—whose name means "mother" in Tamil, Korean, and other languages—is the most maternal being I've ever seen. She opens her arms and pulls each person to her forcefully, whether they're covered in open wounds or wrapped in the most beautiful silk saris money can buy. They don't care about her wisdom or philosophy. They just want to be wrapped in her hugs, to feel love. Her whole being radiates compassion. This is what it means to be a mother, I think. Surrender and sacrifice. I find myself full of emotion as I watch her giving unconditional comfort and love. The room is enveloped in a cocoon of tenderness. It is contagious.

As I sit on stage, jostled by the crowd, a volunteer dressed in white cotton instructs us to make a wish when we're hugged. When my turn comes, I whisper, "I wish to be a mother," as I'm enveloped by Amma's soft, warm flesh. Then she places her lips to my ear and sings a mantra. My eardrum vibrates and the sound takes over my body, and seemingly the whole room. It sounds like "Durga, Durga, Durga."

Durga is a fierce form of the Supreme Goddess, or Mahadevi, manifestation of feminine power in the world. She's a badass war-rior chick, riding on the back of a tiger, eighteen arms holding weapons to slay the most formidable mental demons. Her power embodies every god in the Hindu pantheon. Still buzzing, I stum-ble back through the crowd. Did Amma really give me that man-tra? Does she give it to everyone? Does it matter?

After meeting Amma, I feel empowered. At a sacred place in the realm of an enlightened being, it's easier to remember who we are, to tap into an expansive energy field. I buy a string of wooden prayer beads at the gift shop, to remind me of this moment, of my mantra, of my wish. Then I work my way through the maze of the compound and find our driver, waiting outside. The mantra rings in my ears on the bumpy ride back to the seaside. Hours pass like minutes, and I'm still feeling the bliss, still held in Amma's out-stretched arms, when I return to the retreat and am lulled to sleep by the waves.

The next day, we start the ancient cures. I'm hoping Ayurveda can help me become more fertile. Or if not, at least relax. I meet with the doctor, who explains that in the ancient Indian science, three *doshas*, or elements, maintain the body's balance. Humans are ruled by one *dosha* or some combination of two—or even

three. *Vata* is air, governing movement. *Pitta* is fire, ruling diges-
tion, and *kapha* is earth and water, giving stability. I'm diagnosed
with a *vata* imbalance. Like many urbanites, I have too much nervous energy. I'm too busy and need to get grounded.

To restore my body's balance, the doctor prescribes a daily
treatment of yoga, meditation, and *abhyanga*, a traditional oil massage, for the week. In a coconut-leaf-thatched hut, I sit naked on
a wooden chair while a young woman makes an offering of water,
flowers, and prayers, paints a red *bindi* on my third eye, and waves
incense over me. Covered in sesame oil, I lie face down on a rubber
mat while she holds on to a rope suspended from the ceiling and
digs her feet into my skin, moving in rhythmic strokes to stimulate
my circulation and melt stiff muscles. Then I turn over and she
does it all again.

It's 110 degrees. I sweat out my *vata* in an oily puddle. When
it's over, I'm given a whole coconut to drink from, nectar of the
gods. Breakfast is homemade bread and vegetarian curry. I feel
radiant and relaxed—and it's only the end of the first day. Six
more to go. This is surely heaven, I think.

After my massage, I walk down to the beach. It's still before 8
a.m., and the fishermen are netting small sardine-like fish. There's
also by-catch—scores of blowfish gasping for life, their spiked bodies inflated to fight off danger. They're freed from the nets, but
they're not even thrown back into the sea. In Japan, where I live,
these deadly creatures are a delicacy. They aren't here. Perhaps
the chefs have not learned how to serve them so their poison isn't
ingested.

Hundreds lie along the shore, struggling to breathe. This is
surely hell, I think, as I almost trip over a large one, its sad eyes
fluttering. I tap it lightly with my shoe, try to roll it into the
ocean. But the strong waves send it back to shore again, tumbling
like a stone.

I try to hold it but its spikes stick up. Then it softens—it is weak, or perhaps it feels my intention. So I hurl it into the ocean, watching it try to swim away, hoping it will reach safety. Irrationally, perhaps, I feel strongly that the fish is pregnant. How badly it must want to survive, to lay its eggs. Yet, the forces around it might be too powerful to overcome. I want to stay and watch, to make sure it doesn't get pulled back to shore again, but sheets of rain come down and I have to take refuge inside.

In my hut, I rest and reflect. If I want to welcome a life, I must value all life forms.

Later that night, two more small lives will need attention. I will get my chance.

A bee falls into the honey pot at the dinner table and I scoop it out. A caterpillar is nearly lost in the spray of my shower. I gently intervene, realizing there are hundreds of ways to be a mother, only one of which is to give birth.

Shiva leads us in a juicy, sweaty, passionate yoga practice, then we sit in meditation. I can now honor my desire to be a mother by recognizing all beings as my mother and vowing to repay their kindness.

I sit and watch my breath, trying to transform my desire for a child into a quest to be as mother-like and expansive as possible. It feels right. Besides, at the moment, it's my only option.

From then on, I try my meditation practice with everyone I encounter at the treatment center, try to see them as countless mothers over countless lifetimes. I'm put to the test when the massage therapist asks if I have children—she's half my age and has two. Feelings of shame, then jealousy, arise. I breathe deeply and remember my practice. I watch those feelings surface, let my awareness guide them to another response. She is my mother. She's asking because she loves me. I will repay her kindness.

When the massage is over, I offer her a red envelope stuffed with money for her children.

And, after all these years of being asked that question, I suddenly have an answer that gives me hope.

"Not yet," I say.

At my check-up, the doctor looks at me sympathetically as she tells me about a village where women use their wombs to grow others' babies. "You could go there," she says. I catch myself feeling defensive at her unsolicited advice. Over the years, everyone has a special treatment, diet, doctor, or visualization that has worked for their sister-aunt-friend-second-cousin-twice-removed. None of them has worked for me.

I take a breath, remember: She's my mother. She loves me. She only wants me to be happy.

I thank her for her care. In my mind, I give her a hug. I channel Amma.

Over lunch, I open a newspaper and learn that Amma was attacked the day I visited her ashram. A man had run up to the stage with a knife. The weapon was quickly confiscated, and he was arrested. It happened at 6:45 p.m. Amma didn't want to cause panic, so she didn't stop hugging until five the next morning. The visitors in the back were oblivious; those in the front knew. That's why they'd been so emotional. Amma forgave her attacker, saying, "All those who are born will die one day. I am going ahead keeping this reality in mind."

Everyone is mother.

If I forget this, I'll recall Amma's compassion even for one who might harm her.

Today, as in many days over the years, I ask myself questions many mothers never consider. Why *do* I want to be a mother anyway? I meditate on the answer. I want to experience another kind of love, something beyond what I know or can even imagine. Mother love. I want to experience this kind of earth-shattering, unconditional absoluteness of a mother's love for her child, sent out to anyone and everyone.

The oneness.

I'm starting to feel it. To believe. Everyone is my mother. I am their mother, too.

The next morning's yoga releases more tension, and the meditation brings back a long-buried lesson from the Hebrew school of my youth.

When something doesn't come easy, it's often a test. A test helps us to awaken to and hopefully grow beyond perceived limits. Could my crooked road to motherhood be a test, and could this test be a miracle in itself?

Durga, Durga, Durga.

J A P A N

One Beautiful Egg, 2006

Though I'm hopeful the Ayurvedic treatment has made me healthier and able to conceive, a few months back in Tokyo bring me back to reality.

I go to a fertility clinic in the upscale neighborhood of Omote-Sando. It's reportedly the best clinic in Tokyo. They've even helped the Imperial Family's Crown Princess Masako, who's a year younger than me, get pregnant after eight years of marriage.

The clinic wants to give me the hysterosalpingogram again.

I almost skip it. I've already had the test. But procedure is procedure, and this is Japan.

The dye test shows that both of my tubes are blocked, even though they were open the last time I'd had this test. Well, the right one had been open, and three shots of the dye opened the left one. I still cringe when recalling the sensation.

The clinic puts me on Chlomid and suggests artificial insemination, or IUI.

When that fails, I schedule a laparoscopy to try to open the left tube. In the weeks before the operation, I meditate on opening all the blocked places in myself to allow one little sperm to connect with one little egg and make us a child.

"May the best sperm win," says another yoga teacher, Jennifer, who has been married just one year and is already seven months pregnant.

She doesn't know our history, and I don't tell her.

Instead, I just sigh. And then I sigh some more.

On operation day, they test all my vitals. It turns out I have an irregular heartbeat, a very slow pulse, and a condition called bradycardia—an extremely slow heart rate, which yoga makes even slower. I've known about the bradycardia since childhood, but it's never caused any problems. In fact, some say a slow heart rate means a long life—like an elephant or a turtle. Now, I'm not so sure.

I'm stripped, laid on a table, put under. They cut open my belly, pump gas in to blow it up like a giant beach ball. Then they get in and try to untwist the tubes. Many hours later, the result is mixed. They can only untwist one. The other is so wound up around itself that it cannot be untangled, like the trunk of an ancient bonsai tree, growing in its stunted way.

It takes me a long time to "come to," the anesthesiologist says, due to the heartrate. The doctors are worried. But when I'm back, the doctor tells me I have a beautiful egg.

"Very good condition for your age," he says pleasantly, as if complimenting my skin or my cooking.

"Huh?" I say, still groggy.

"There's a good egg on your right side, but we can't harvest it," he says, looking at me with sad eyes.

"I tried, but couldn't."

I'm heartened by this news. At least I still had an egg. And the condition was good. I know Japanese doctors are famous for not telling the truth about cancer so as to "protect" the patient from reality. Could this be the reverse? He wouldn't lie to me, would he?

My friends remain positive, saying, "You can still get pregnant with one tube."

But it's time to get real. I'm over forty now.

IVF is the only option I haven't pursued, and sensationalistic news stories about sixty-five-year-old women giving birth through IVF aside, it's getting down to the wire.

So I go to the clinic. They test my Follicle Stimulating Hormone, which is a measure of fertility, and it's low for my age, due to all the Chinese herbs I've been sucking down. That means we can proceed. As is their protocol, they put me on the pill. Then they test my FSH again in a month, and it's shot up to an unacceptably high number. Why? I've never been on the pill before; my body is sensitive. And the high FSH is normal for someone like me. Someone old.

The doctor sucks in his breath and folds his hands over his chest. He leans back in his chair and tells me my eggs are too old, that IVF will probably fail.

"I'd like to try anyway," I say.

To my surprise, the clinic flat-out refuses.

Perhaps they don't want to add more failures to their statistical success rate. In America, I think, they'd keep taking your money until you ran out.

But here, the doctor says no.

"Don't waste your money, time, or energy."

And that is that.

"What are her options?" Shogo asks anyway, catching my dejected look.

"She could always try a donor egg," the doctor says, shuffling papers on his desk and glancing up at the clock.

There's just one problem. Donor eggs are illegal in Japan.

Water Children

I go to the temple of Jizo in Shiba Park to say a prayer for my unborn child.

Jizo stands tall in his red apron and red cap with his pilgrim's staff in his hands.

His eyes have no pupils, and in this way, it is said, he can see and not-see. I gaze into the no-seeing, all-seeing eyes, wondering how they see everything and nothing, inside and outside, the world and the non-world, dust and ether and sky.

Jizo is the patron saint of departed children. He guards their souls as they travel over the Sanzu River into the netherworld. Sometimes he's depicted as a child himself, a pilgrim carrying a staff with six jingling rings to announce his friendly approach.

He's the guardian spirit of *mizuko*, the souls of stillborn, miscarried, or aborted fetuses, or children who died very young.

Here, hundreds of Jizo statues stand silently in rows. I bow down to them, placing my hands in prayer at my heart, and try to find some quiet space inside, some space beyond the internal chatter and the external noise. I try to enter a space of limitless potential, limitless kindness and compassion. I try to find the space of letting go of the outcome.

I pray for the children's safety, and my own.

Being there soothes me, gives me a place to put my grief, to get it out of my body.

Looking down, I see that it's a well-traveled path. Stones and pebbles are piled up near the statues, put there by parents in the belief that this might lessen the amount of suffering their children endure in the underworld. The Jizos wear tiny red clothes, hats, and bibs. Pinwheels, toys, and stuffed animals surround them, placed as offerings to the god to protect their children's passage. There's a ritual called *mizuko kuyo*, an offering to water children. I ladle water from the nearby stone trough onto the statues, washing them as I wash away my tears.

Pregnant women also pray to Jizo, but most women, like me, come to ritualize their loss, to give it a place to rest.

I release my sadness to Jizo, and my pain subsides. My womb can't bear fruit, but can my mind? Can my imagination give birth to stories, breathe life into characters, build worlds and inhabit them with people? If I can't give birth to a child, can I write myself into being?

I want to find the fertile fruit of words and explore the deepest, juiciest seeds I can unearth within. I want to rewrite my story.

On some primal level, I understand that my family life is my first story, my first narrative I tell about myself. Our narrators are always unreliable, in a sense, because we filter experience through our own belief systems. Yet our minds and memories are the only witnesses we have. I know enough to know that things aren't always what they seem, and that my story isn't over.

The more I meditate and practice yoga, the more I determine to rewrite my childhood scenes, to edit how I frame them in my mind. I decide to view the challenges as lessons, the difficult people as teachers.

I decide to focus on all the things I'm grateful for, and there are many—my mother taught me how to read, and what a gift that is! My father instilled in me a love of music and beauty. He always gave me roses from his garden.

Now they make genetically engineered roses without thorns. How strange is that, to have a rose without thorns?

Regret

Peggy sends an email, short and straight, like a one-two punch. She's been diagnosed with pancreatic cancer, stage four. There is no hope.

"At least I can spend the last few months of my life in a dream," she writes. "I can look out at the ocean and know that I am but a small speck on the earth."

Not to me.

Peggy is my life. At thirty-five, she'd had uterine cancer followed by a hysterectomy and had been unable to have children. She'd thought about adoption, but had never pursued it. The one thing she regretted, she said, was that she never had a child. At fifty-five, she retired from social work.

Now, at sixty-one, she's facing death. I'm devastated. The news of her condition catapults me back into action. I consider trying another clinic, but Shogo thinks we should respect the doctor's honest opinion based on how I've reacted to the drugs so far. There are lots of reasons not to try IVF at this point, such as ovarian cancer, which is a side effect of the drugs for IVF, and a high rate of ovarian cysts. Shogo and the doctor both think I should give up.

I am not someone who gives up easily.

Shogo reminds me that walking away from the fight is a sign of strength, not weakness. Throwing down your sword is a way to take back your power.

Faith

Kausthub Desikachar, grandson of the Hatha yoga legend Krish-namacharya—considered the "father" of modern *vinyasa* yoga—comes to Tokyo. After taking lessons with him, his mother and father, I have a private yoga therapy session at his hotel. He asks what my "issue" is. I describe my struggle to conceive a child. Then I tell him all I've been doing about it.

He sits back in his chair, fingers tented, considering my words.

He looks at me askance, takes a deep breath.

"What do you need me for? It seems you know what to do," he says.

"I don't," I insist. I want reassurance, perhaps some tradi-tional wisdom, anything to give me hope. That's it, I realize. I want *hope*.

I tell him that.

"Okay, then," he says, smiling widely. Then he gives me a practice and a mantra in the traditional combination—chanting as you move. He tells me that a Japanese student will teach me a chant to help me "open my womb."

Later, he sends me a letter entitled "Faith in Healing," about an experience his grandfather had with a student in her thirties who'd wanted to have a child.

> The woman told him of her inability to conceive a child, and said that this was threatening her marriage, as her husband was threatening to leave her for another woman. I knew that it was (and still is) very important in many Asian countries to see a continued lineage.
>
> Krishnamacharya gave her a yoga sequence and traditional medication made from ash to be mixed with honey, and blessed her and the mixture with an invocation to the sun. He told her to do the practice and take the medication every day, then try to conceive after thirty days A few months later, she returned, pregnant. She thanked her teacher for healing her.
>
> Krishnamacharya replied, "It is not I who has healed you. It is your faith and your disciplined practice that has healed you. Had you not had faith in me or the practice, you would not have been healed."
>
> The Sanskrit word for faith is sraddha from the root dha, to hold or sustain.
>
> Faith will hold us, though alone, it is not enough. One also must practice, as instructed by one's teacher.
>
> A simple reason my grandfather would insist on faith is due to the fact that "Healing is a journey that has to be patiently pursued."
>
> Healing takes months, years. Faith is what sustains our practice over this long period and helps us fight discouragement at the apparent lack of healing. We need faith and commitment to give us strength to trust the process.

*At this moment I understand why the ancient
masters laid such importance on the role of faith.*
*This is how Krishmamacharya healed so many
people—by igniting their faith. This is how he healed
himself.*

It's a very beautiful letter and a profound statement, and I'm happy for the woman. Yet, the letter touches a nerve. I have faith and always have had faith, but I can't get pregnant—and there are thousands of women just like me. The implication is that with faith, you can work miracles. But the logic also implies that if you fail, you must be somehow lacking faith.

I know with all my heart that faith is not something I lack. Perhaps, however, my faith is too one-pointed. Perhaps I need to expand my faith to trust that this voice I hear is real, that it is leading me to my child, and that I just have to keep opening doors until I find the one he's hiding behind. Maybe I've been looking in the wrong places. Maybe the miracle will not look like what I think it will.

I commit to practicing the routine Kausthub has given me for thirty-one days, though it takes two hours and requires memorization of a very long mantra and precise Sanskrit pronunciation to work. No matter. I'm down.

I'll try anything.

Failing Forward

Kausthub's student Sachiyo comes over to teach me proper Vedic pronunciation for the mantra that reportedly nurtures the flowering of the feminine. In the week since I've seen Kausthub, I've chanted it daily while visualizing water in my womb. I feel softer, lighter already.

I brew some organic *hojicha*. Sachiyo and I sip it and talk about the sequence. Then we go into my mother-in-law's teahouse, where Sachiyo teaches me the proper Sanskrit tones so that I can raise my "mother vibration." The proper tones will invite more peace, calm, and acceptance into my life.

"Show me how you've been doing it," she says.

I do the routine, going through the paces.

I finish, look over at her expectantly.

She bites her lip, as if considering whether she should say what she thinks, or be Japanese and hold back. She knows that holding back won't help me.

"You don't have to be forceful about it. Leave some space for joy," she says.

At first, I feel defensive, but then I realize she's right. I've been barreling my way through the sequence, fueled by the unconscious belief that the harder I work at it, the more chance it has of being effective. *Same old, same old. My go-to survival mode.*

"You're right," I agree. I need to step back, surrender, soften. "It needs more joy. Thank you," I say.

I practice the sequence and mantra for thirty-one days, softly and joyfully. It's a beautiful prayer to the flower, the feminine, the womb. The movements open my pelvis, make my throat soft, my heart open.

The next month, my period is late. Could Krishnamacharya's ancient yoga practice finally be what I've hoped for?

I try not to feel too happy, or hopeful, or expectant.

But I can't help it. I'm excited. My period hasn't been late for years.

The excitement is, of course, short-lived. Two weeks later,

blood comes. I try not to blame myself. The lateness is probably a residual effect of the hormone shots.

Still, I keep at the practice.

I hold my faith. I submit to that which is beyond my control.

I give myself until December to keep trying.

Month after month, I joyfully fail.

Letting Go

December comes, and along with it, my period.

I dream constantly of our child, our beautiful child. I wonder where he or she is.

I had faith that it would happen naturally, once I healed myself and unblocked my blocks. I was sure my miracle would come.

But now I know that miracles take many forms.

Maybe it was because I'd opened the yoga studio and was supposed to "mother" the students who went there. If I had a child of my own, I'd certainly be too busy.

I think of a long list of reasons.

Perhaps I am being protected somehow.

Maybe I couldn't get pregnant because having a child or giving birth would be too risky for my heart. Maybe I would die in childbirth, and the child would, too.

Then I stop my mind from these endless wanderings. Mainly, I just try to be grateful for all that I have.

When the list exhausts itself, I know it's time to let go. Just accept it. Be with what is.

There are thousands of happy childless couples, many by choice. And there are thousands of other ways to be a mother in the world. Peggy taught me that.

I go into the closet and take out the box my sister Amy gave me when we left California. The baby clothes smell musty, look rumpled and sad. I shake out little hoodies, small shoes, caps. They smell like my nephew, or rather, how he smelled when he was a baby. He's eight years old now.

I fold down the flaps and carry the box downstairs.

I donate the clothes to the Salvation Army, where I hope that someone with a child can find them and use them.

AMERICA

The Samurai Spirit

For my birthday, my mother offers her timeshare in Hawaii. I haven't taken a vacation with her since I was a teenager. Hawaii is halfway between Japan and America, and it's a good place to meet. I had good luck there before in Haiku. Maybe the island will lead me to a miracle again.

The minute I get off the plane and walk through the garden court of the Honolulu Airport, the smell of freshly cut grass and the rich fragrance of plumeria and jasmine permeate the air and make me feel at ease.

It is so nice to have clean, fresh air—even at an airport. And grass. Something I never used to notice, but now miss, living in Tokyo.

My mother and I walk the beach, do yoga together. I work in Fish Pose, Camel, Plow. I open my throat, release the chokehold. I honor my words, my truth. I keep a journal.

I feel soothed by the ocean breeze, the rainforests, the lushness of it all. We talk about the past. When I was younger, we fought a lot. There was much about her struggle I didn't understand. Like why she didn't take me with her when she left. Why she couldn't. She says she's sorry for all the mistakes she made, the things she did and didn't do. I say the same.

Now I see that my mother acted selflessly most of the time. With limited resources, she thought of my sisters and me, wanted us to be happy, to have a better future than she had had.

It's good to feel that we can meet each other here and now. Just where we are.

I meditate. I listen for the voice I heard years before on this island, urging me to open the yoga studio in Tokyo. Will it give me wise counsel again?

All it says is: *Let go, let go, let go.*

I've almost left my grief behind, I think, when we tour a bird sanctuary. The ranger tells us of the Hawaiian national bird, the nene (Hawaiian goose), who chooses a mate just to build a family.

"If the female doesn't reproduce," she says matter-of-factly, "the male quickly dumps her and moves on."

My mother looks at me, sadly.

I glance away. But I know that what the ranger has said is right. In the end, it's all about survival and reproduction. It's just basic Darwinism.

"You're a fighter," Shogo's mother once told me. "You have the samurai spirit."

Be that as it may, I know that the samurai spirit also embodies an acceptance of failure, usually at the sharp end of a sword.

When one has tried one's best, failure is noble, dignified.

I hold up my head, try to be dignified.

I try to embody the samurai spirit.

Just keep me away from anything sharp.

Clean and Clear

Dietmar the psychic comes to Tokyo again. It's been seven years since I first visited him in Harajuku.

"What happened to you?" he asks, shaking out his hand like he's touched fire.

"Nothing," I say, and then reconsider. "Everything."

"You got younger. Your entire body changed. And your energy body, too!"

"Really? Maybe it's the yoga," I reply. I tell him about the studio, Shogo, everything.

We talk for a while about this and that. Then he straightens up, gets serious.

"So where's your child?" he asks.

"I don't know."

He looks me up and down. "Look. You're totally clean and clear. I can't see or feel any blockages. Your child should be here."

Try as I might, I can't stop the tears from welling up.

"You've done so much work, It's not like you not to pursue something to the fullest. When you want something, you go after it. Why haven't you gone after this?"

"I have," I say. "I thought I could do it naturally. I thought instead of pushing and striving, I could surrender and trust."

"How's that been working for you?" he asks.

"Like shit," I acknowledge.

"Right," he laughs.

"I've seen this child around you for years. And I see that you have gone deep and released the pain. And you have forgiven. Bravo."

"So what now?" I ask.

"All I can say is that maybe your child doesn't want to come into the world as it is now. Sometimes I see this. A soul comes when it wants to come. . . . But your child does not like this world. Who would want to come into this world? There's so much pain, and sadness."

"But there's also great beauty and joy."

"Yes. So you will have to get rid of this conditioning, this almost biblical condemnation of yourself as a barren woman, cast out into the desert. Like Sarah in the Bible, or something."

I bristle at this comment.

"I don't consider myself a barren woman," I say.

"Good. Then prove it," he challenges me. "Think of so many women who give birth but have no real heart connection to their children. You see, it's not always about giving birth from your body."

The wheels start to turn in my mind. I nod, urging him on.

"What I am saying is that this child is not going to come from your womb. But it will come from your heart. Which is more important?"

"I can't stand to get my hopes up again," I say as tears roll down my face.

"Release your conditioning," he says, handing me a tissue. "Your child is coming."

I bawl like a blubbering wreck.

"He will come. And he will be a beautiful child," he says.

"I want to believe you, but I've tried, and . . ."

"You'll need to fight for this one. You'll need to fight for it, tooth and nail."

"Big surprise," I say. "Story of my life."

"So what!" he says, waving his hand in the air. "You're a war-rior. You're a fighter. Of course that's the path you're going to walk on. Stop being a victim!"

Again, I bristle. But only because once again, he's struck a chord.

"See the magic around you. Wake up. Take the reins."

"Okay, okay," I say, encouraged. His enthusiasm is contagious. And maybe, just maybe, he really does see something.

"Are you writing about this?" he asks.

I sigh. "I don't know. It's so personal," I say. "And I don't want to hurt anyone around me."

"Phshaw," he says. "You hurt yourself by holding it in. Tell your story. If anyone's hurt, it's because they recognize the truth. And, it could help someone."

His eyes move to the garnet necklace. It's resting on my fifth chakra. The place of self-expression, of speaking your truth.

"Just write for yourself," he says.

"I'll try."

"Don't *try*. Do it. Promise?"

"Promise."

"Good. Now go out and find that child."

SIXTH CHAKRA

From the Sanskrit term meaning "to perceive," or "to know." The sixth chakra is the third-eye chakra, located in the brain but often depicted between the eyebrows on the forehead. The element is light.

When this chakra is balanced, you trust your intuition, are able to see the "big picture," and are able to connect, communicate with, and trust the Higher Self. This chakra is considered the center of inner wisdom, wisdom, and individuality. Development of this chakra cultivates the "sixth sense"—intuition, visions, dreams. It is also known as the "*guru* (teacher) chakra."

Adoption

I go online and research adoption in Japan. I discover that the adoption of adults is common practice for financial or business reasons, but adoption of children is rare, perhaps unsurprisingly. Japan is notoriously closed about the process. There's not much information available, and what is out there doesn't look promising. The wait could take years, without any guarantee. Mainly the number of waiting children is small compared to other countries. Foreigners are outsiders, so the chances of a successful placement seem slim, even with a Japanese partner. People do manage to adopt here, though. Still, I don't think I can handle the disappointment.

I talk it over with Shogo. Perhaps other countries will be easier, he agrees. So I search "international adoption" and discover that there are hundreds of agencies and dozens of countries to potentially adopt from. Since I'm already in Asia, I look to China, South Korea.

But when I consider the reality of adopting a child from any of these countries, I don't feel as strong of a connection. If we were to adopt a child from China or South Korea, we'd want to have some ties—friends or family from those countries to connect with, if possible.

Then there is Vietnam. I think about it. My relationship to that country is tinged by war, just as my parents' relationship to Japan is tinged by war. I remember that my friend Duc, a former radio broadcaster who I worked with in San Francisco, now lives in Hanoi. I feel close to Duc and his family, and which makes Vietnam feel closer, less of an unknown.

I contact a dozen agencies. Most don't write back. The few who do respond weeks or months later say they don't work with families who live "abroad." Their applications ask questions like: Why do you want a child? How do you feel about birth mothers? (I notice they don't ask about birth fathers.) One even asks about the first time the adoptive parent had sex.

The questions irk me. Is this information really necessary or relevant?

I take a deep breath. This is my process. *In some way, I chose this,* I tell myself.

Finally, I find a private agency that handles adoptions in Japan, fill out the form, email it in. The next week, they write back. After accepting our initial application, it will cost two thousand dollars to file a secondary application. The process will take about two years, during which time we'll be on a waiting list. *If* there's a placement, the child will be older, but they can't guarantee a placement.

Shogo and I think it through. Due to our ages, cut-off dates for adoption are rapidly approaching. We can't afford to wait two years, especially with no guarantee on the other end.

We decide to pursue adoption in Vietnam and send in for an application.

Starstruck, September 2006

The Head Teacher at Sun and Moon, Em, sometimes gets paperbacks and tabloids like *Hello* and *Us* from one of the students. Em passes them on to me. They're ideal for going somewhere completely mindless for a few precious hours.

One autumn week, there's an article about Angelina Jolie and Brad Pitt, who are planning to adopt a little boy from Vietnam. The article mentions Dr. Jane Aronson, a woman who helps people with foreign adoptions.

I google Dr. Aronson and read with admiration about the work she is doing with orphans around the world. She has adopted two children herself.

I email her asking for referrals, not really expecting a reply. To my surprise, she answers my email me right away (she's online at the same time!) and gives me the names of two agencies who work in international adoptions for people living abroad. And this is a busy woman, a famous woman, an amazing woman.

I write back immediately, thanking her for being there, for helping me, for hearing me, for acknowledging my existence.

She emails me right back again.

You will adopt. You will move on, she writes.

Thank you, I write back, sobbing into the keyboard.

Thank you.

First Steps

I write to the agencies Dr. Aronson recommends. Meanwhile, my friend Jacinta gives me the name of an Australian psychologist who's adopted an infant in Japan through the government agency's Child Guidance Center—Jido Sodan Jo. There are offices in each of Tokyo's twenty-three wards, established under the Child Welfare Law.

The CGC offers free counseling for issues concerning children under eighteen. Anyone—the child, family members, school teachers, local residents—can use their services, which range from help with questions on childrearing to dealing with stress and anger management, school problems, and other educational issues.

More serious problems like abuse, neglect, domestic violence, and human rights concerns also go to the CGC.

The CGC also handles child adoptions. That year, 2006, around thirty thousand children under the age of eighteen live in welfare facilities. In Tokyo, four thousand children are not living within a family unit. In 2004, family courts recognized only 322 adoptions of children under the age of six, and 998 adoptions of children over six.

That's 1,320 adoptions, with less than half of those between children and parents who have no blood connection. In other words, most adoptions are still within the family.

In the U.S., there are approximately 127,000 annual adoptions. 1.7 million households have an adopted child.

In Japan, there's a long-standing stigma about adoption, a reluctance of birth parents or extended family to relinquish legal claim to a child, even when they cannot take care of it. Most adoptions are kept secret. Some children don't even find out they're adopted until their parents die.

On top of that, there is the traditional importance of family history and the *koseki* (family register), which lists every birth, marriage, and divorce. Bloodlines are seen as all-important; one's ancestors are one's link to the past. The *koseki* goes back generations and lists each birth and marriage, tying family to family.

When Shogo and I got married, keeping my own name had created a problem with the *koseki*. And regarding adoptive families, it was not until 1988 that the law allowed a child's birth and family name to be erased from the birth parent's *koseki* and be replaced by the adoptive parents' name.

There are private agencies that specialize in adoption, but the process takes many years and can cost anywhere from twenty to sixty thousand dollars. Public adoption through the CGC is free.

If a child is placed, the family receives a small monthly stipend from the government to help with costs.

We decide to visit the CGC, though the odds are daunting. To add to the challenge, of course, everything must be discussed in Japanese. I appreciate that Shogo is a translator and that he has the patience of a saint. I also appreciate that in some ways I am probably only going to catch half of what is happening. So I won't know how much I am up against, and that's a definite plus.

Shogo and I go to the Shinagawa Ward office, the same one we were married at, to fill out an initial application. We answer another round of questions:

> Why do you want a child?
> What kind of upbringing and education would you give your child?
> What are the most important values you would share with a child?
> What about religion?

Filling out the application is challenging, but it's an opportunity to become clear on what our values are and what kind of parents we see ourselves as being. We talk about issues most parents don't address until they come up, if then. It feels good to sort these things out in advance in a calm, organized way. Just the same, having these discussions pulls at my heartstrings. Will Shogo and I ever just get to be parents?

We cross our fingers and wait.

I email Peggy, who's thrilled. I call my mother and tell her we've begun the adoption process. She tells me there's precedent in Jewish history. Pharaoh's daughter, Batiah, rescued baby

Moses from a basket floating down the Nile and raised him as her son. King David's wife, Michal, raised her sister's five sons. Mordechai fostered his orphaned cousin Esther, and so on.

Although none of the biblical adoptions of legend were recognized by Halakhah, Jewish law, my mother has fitted this adoption into our Jewish life narrative, making sense of it in a way she can live with.

I can live with that, too.

Bloodlines

Slowly and with caution, we begin to tell our friends that we're hoping to adopt. Partly it's to ease the pain of the constant barrage of questions such as "When are you having kids?" Or "Why don't you have children yet?"

But next we have to deal with lots of opinions and more careless comments. People, it turns out, have strong opinions on adoption, especially people who have naturally born children.

"Oh, we'd love to adopt too, some day," or "We considered adoption, too. . . ."

And so on.

One thing everyone agrees on is this: Japan is a difficult country to adopt from. We brace ourselves and take the next step—gaining permission.

Asking your husband's parents for his hand in marriage is rare in the modern world, but getting permission from your in-laws to have a child is virtually unheard of. Yet that's exactly what we have to do.

Neither Shogo nor I had asked for permission to marry, nor did we tell our parents until after our civil service. In years past, new brides needed in-laws' approval to enter into the *koseki*. After the war, newlyweds could make their own.

But keeping my maiden name had been problematic. The *koseki* had no place for "outside" names. Shogo had insisted, and space was made.

That was that, or so I thought, until now, twelve years later, when I have to ask my father-in-law for permission to have a child. Shogo's sisters have already said yes. It's his father I am worried about. Though it's more of an unspoken law than an official one, Japan is one of the only countries in the world that require extended family approval if the adopting family is Japanese. Inner—or *uchi*—is paramount in Japan. Family is *uchi*. Outside (*soto*) is secondary. The social worker told us that a recent placement fell through when a grandmother didn't approve. They are extra careful to get the entire extended family's agreement.

For the purposes of our application, Shogo's father consented.

Then my real worries began.

If we succeeded in adoption, I'd be bucking the system again. Though the *koseki* system has changed, Japan is still feudal in its worship of bloodlines. Most adoptions are kept secret. In Japan, family and appearances matter deeply, and while my own beliefs differ, it is Japanese beliefs that will shape my child's experiences. In this, outside (*soto*) reveals its true force.

I know foreign women who do not take their half-Japanese children to school; the kids are embarrassed that their mothers are different from everyone else's. If we adopt, the child won't look like me, so everyone will know. He could be a victim of *ijime*, bullying. This could lead to *hikikomori*—refusal to leave the house. Or worse, *jisatsu*—suicide. I know I am being neurotic, already thinking about the difficulties a then-unknown child could face. I know I am already being a mother.

I share my fears with Shogo. He reminds me we are a rainbow family, he with his long hair and stay-at-home job, me with my funky yoga studio. In a conservative neighborhood in a homogenous country, we already stand out. Why not embrace our differences completely?

We are optimistic about our chances for adoption, although the odds are slim, especially considering the small number of adoptions in Japan each year. Plus, I am forty-four, Shogo is forty-eight. Our ages make us low priority. I figure, if I'm lucky, I have around ten thousand days left to live. How do I want to spend them? I want a family, I want a child. Though I love Shogo deeply, I want my world to be bigger than just us two.

Besides that, we have nothing to lose.

When our application is approved, I am overjoyed, and surprised.

Could our dream finally be coming true?

Low Priority

We attend an all-day lecture with fifty other couples who are hoping to adopt—and those are only applicants for this season. Hundreds of others have previously applied and are waiting.

I try not to think about this as we prepare to visit Nazareth House, an orphanage in Takadanobaba, a university district. Before our trip, we go to Kiddieland—a bustling three-story toy shop in Harajuku not far from the salon where Dietmar had made his prediction.

The store is a cacophony of bells, whistles, motors, and mechanized voices. It gives me a headache. I buy finger puppets—the most low-tech thing there. I'm surprised the shop even has them.

We plan to take the puppets to the orphanage, to bring something inconspicuous and quiet.

We arrive and check in. It's a cluster of fenced-in wooden buildings painted white, with an astro-turf playground in the center of a courtyard. For reasons I can't quite pinpoint, the place looks and feels like a small-town American church, circa 1950. I try not to look at the other couples in the meeting room too carefully, try to stay focused on the lecture in Japanese on life in the orphanage.

A woman explains how the kids there are accustomed to institutional ways, and are different from kids who grow up in "normal" families. A few minutes in, I find myself looking around the room at the other potential adoptive parents. Each of them has a journey, a story like ours. Some are much younger than us, dressed in hip clothes. Others look older, more conservative. Many, like us, seem to have long-term marriages. I can tell by the way they relate, hopeful but wary. They've been on a long journey.

When lunch is over, the kids can play in the playground. The staff lets the prospective parents out to the playground for ten minutes, all as a group.

At first, it is uncomfortable. How are we supposed to appear relaxed when the staff are watching us? And the kids, what must they think of these strange people who are suddenly let in to "play" with them?

Some of the couples are hesitant, moving slowly toward the children, with a mixture of hope and fear. We're one of them.

I step back and look at myself from the child's point of view.

I see what they see. We are strangers. We are *strange*. I'd be scared too.

Waiting. Wanting. Just like us.

I notice another group of kids playing on the other side of the playground, riding swings or taking turns going down the slide, chasing each other. Two harried-looking women do their best to keep an eye on the twenty kids, ages two to five.

A shy little girl hides in the corner. Her bright clothes are rumpled, and she reminds me of Raggedy Ann. There is something off-kilter about her, but it's something interesting, not sad or resigned. I realize what it is: she is watching, paying attention. She is *present*. Her eyes are not half-dead, already tuned out like some of the others. She is curious. She notices me looking at her and shyly goes to hide behind a pole.

A big, strong boy runs around terrorizing the others. Another boy, who appears to be half-Japanese and half Middle-Eastern, won't stop crying.

I approach the ball cabinet, take out a striped rubber ball and throw it to Shogo. He catches it, throws it back. We do this a few times. Some of the kids take notice and move closer to us. Eventually, we throw the ball to them. They throw it back to us. We're in a circle.

A few go into the ball cabinet and try to retrieve more balls, but the balls are in the back. One boy climbs in and hits his head on the sharp metal shelf as he tries to climb out of the cabinet while keeping the ball in his hands. A staff member frowns and says, "That shelf is dangerous! Please watch him!"

"Yes," I say. "Sorry!" I feel chastised and chagrined. I've already done something wrong.

Shogo beckons to the boy, who takes a shy step, then falls flat on his face. Now he cries for real. I want to approach him, but I know he'll be scared, which will make him cry more. The woman rushes up and scoops him up in her arms. She doesn't say anything. She doesn't have to. I sense her disapproval.

The super-sized boy darts over.

"Think quick!" I say, shooting him the ball. He doesn't catch it, but laughs uproariously and goes off to chase it. He comes back, throws it to Shogo.

I throw the ball to the Middle Eastern boy, too, but he just sits and cries.

He looks so sad, so defeated.

I think: *Could I love him? Could he someday be my son? And if I were his mom, could he love me back?*

Falling through the Cracks

Weeks go by. We attend more lectures, including a sobering talk from a man who's waited ten years to get a placement from CGC and ended up fostering two older children who'd been in the system since birth. Their parents wouldn't legally relinquish them but couldn't afford to care for them at home. So many others live in foster-care facilities, in limbo.

He relates how their birth parents were supposed to come for Christmas and the kids were so excited they stayed up all night, waited all day. The birth parents never showed up. The kids ran away.

Another woman talks about a boy she fostered, who at seven still wet his pants. He really, really wanted to get out of diapers, so he tried his best to wear training pants, only to wet them too and chastise himself daily for his failure.

My heart goes out to these children and to the people who foster them.

What will happen to them? Will they be reunited with their birth parents after the families have overcome their financial hardships? Or will they be stuck in the foster care system forever until they get sent out into the world on their eighteenth birthdays?

And then what? Will society help them, or will they continue to fall through the cracks?

Though I understand the reasoning behind the desire to keep the family "intact," this is not what happens to such children. They are wards of the court, with no families to speak of. They sit and languish in orphanages while hundreds of couples wait futilely, their dreams of adopting never materializing.

I want to adopt them all, give them all families.

But I can't. I'll be lucky if I can even adopt one.

Guidelines

Every step of the adoption process feels daunting. The following guidelines are for prospective parents filing for a special adoption:

(1) The child must be under the age of six at the time the adoption petition is filed OR under the age of eight, and must have been placed under the continuous care and custody of the prospective adoptive parents since before the child's sixth birthday.

(2) Two adoptive parents must jointly consent to the adoption. Single parents may only pursue a special adoption with the Family Court's consent.

(3) One of the adoptive parents must be over twenty-five years of age and the other must be over twenty years old.

(4) All persons with legal custody of the child, including the natural and adoptive parents, must consent to the adoption, EXCEPT IF:

> (a) the natural parents are incapable of declaring their intent,
>
> (b) Family Court rules that the natural parents have treated the child with "cruelty,"
>
> (c) the natural parents have abandoned the child, or
>
> (d) any other cause "seriously harmful to the benefits of the person to be adopted" exists.

(5) The child must be in the custody of, and residing with, the adoptive parents for at least six months before the Family Court will render a final judgment and issue an adoption decree.

I have to read the passage around ten times before I can read it all the way through without my head spinning. And that's after it's been translated into English!

"You sure you want to do this?" Shogo asks.

"I'm sure," I say.

He takes a deep breath. "What if nothing happens? Can you handle it?"

The truth is, I don't know. But we've come this far.

And I'm an American samurai, not one to give up easily.

"If nothing happens, then we'll be right where we are now," I reply.

Giving and Taking

At the yoga studio, I invite students to dedicate their practice to people who are suffering. We try to take away their pain through Tonglen, the Tibetan Buddhist practice of "giving and taking."

I've been practicing it on my own and decide to guide them through it. If we want to change ourselves, we have to change our minds as well as our bodies, our hearts as well as our minds. Tonglen is one of the best methods I know of cracking open the heart.

So I guide them through the meditation, and we practice taking away someone else's pain—breathing it in and giving them healing and happiness by sending the wish for their happiness.

In the meditation, we picture people we know—our fathers, mothers, ancestors—and see them in pain. With each breath, we imagine taking the pain into our hearts, transforming it with love in an explosion of light, destroying it forever.

Then we send them the wish for happiness and freedom, and shower them with anything that will make them happy. We make an offering of this wish—sending them their favorite foods, their loved ones, a beautiful sunset. Whatever they love.

Once we can hold our concentration, this is not so difficult. It's a joy to help those we love and care for. Then we send those who've hurt us the wish for happiness. This is a bit more challenging.

Next, we picture people we barely know—someone who has served us in a cafe, or the bus driver, or someone across us in a crowded train, and again, we hit blocks and walls. Can we care about someone we don't know at all, barely even notice? Can we take on their pain and suffering?

Lastly, we practice taking in all the pain in the world, and transforming it into happiness. Little by little, we find that our own lives become happier and somehow free.

I cannot teach what I don't practice. I have to practice and practice and practice.

I meditate more to open my sixth chakra—the place of inner knowing, deep wisdom, intuition. During this time, I try to sit with the uncertainty.

In my meditations and in my yoga practice, I try to listen within.

At the studio, I have the students do Sun Salutations blindfolded so they don't look outward. So they can look, and listen, to the teacher within.

It's unnerving, and powerful. How much of what we do is dictated by what we're told, or what's expected of us, or what we think others will approve of?

I put the blindfold on myself. I forge onward, keeping my ears tuned to that faint inner voice that gets louder and louder in the listening.

I keep my ears open for the voice of my child.

A Child Who Requires Protection

The following month, we return to the orphanage. This time, on the way in, we see a handsome Iranian man dressed in a three-piece suit. He's young, maybe twenty-four, and looks like a prince. I am astonished when I see the half–Middle Eastern boy who was crying incessantly last time we visited emerge from behind the fence and take the man's hand.

Clearly, it is the boy's biological father. For whatever reason, he isn't able to take care of the boy at home. Still, he's come to visit. Maybe he comes often. Maybe this is the first time, or the last; I will never know.

It's the first time I have seen one of the birth parents, and I can't take my eyes off him.

"Stop staring," Shogo whispers.

I shake my head. I can't help it.

"Daddy," the little boy says, over and over and over. He's smiling.

I look at my husband, tears in my eyes.

I find out later (because I do the American thing and ask) that he is one of the many children in the orphanage who is *not* up for adoption. He is kept there indefinitely until his parents' circumstances change. If they change.

He is luckier than some. Some of the biological parents never visit their children. Yet the law does not release them to be adopted by waiting parents.

They are not "adoptable children," or in legal terms, "children who require protection."

In Japan, an "adoptable child" is "a minor who has been irrevocably released for adoption by its sole surviving parent, by a legal guardian, by both parents (if both parents are living and remain married), by the natural mother (in the case of an out-of-wedlock birth), or by the institution that has custody of the child."

Under Japanese law, a child can be adopted in one of two ways: regular and special.

Regular adoption is when the child is a descendant of one of the adoptive parents. The City Office registers a regular adoption with or without the Family Court's consent.

Special Adoption severs the child's ties to the birth parents. Most children placed through CGC are special adoptions.

I wonder if the shy girl with the crooked bangs who hides in the corner is going to spend the rest of her childhood in the orphanage.

If so, I wish I could visit her daily. But there are strict rules and regulations. I am lucky to be here now.

On this visit, our second, a smile creeps from the corners of her mouth.

She comes over to play. Eventually, she lets me push her on the swing. Before I know it, she is smiling broadly, and has almost climbed onto my lap.

I look at her sweet fragile face. Again, the thought arises:

Could I love this girl? Could she be my daughter?

Soon, she is completely on my lap.

What lonely kids really want is to be picked up and held, even if they don't know it.

They want touch. It's what lonely adults want, too.

I wrap my arms around her.

The boys crowd around Shogo, pulling on his leg. He has to lift them all up one by one. They wait in line for it, because when he lifts one kid up, they don't want to be put back down.

Finally, the staff tells us it's time to go inside.

I pass the Middle Eastern boy as we leave. He's crying again, his father is gone.

When our hour is up, we go to a nearby Indian restaurant for lunch with an Australian couple who have also applied to be adoptive parents. They say they already have three kids "of their own," but they want to adopt two more to have a bigger family.

I wrestle with my emotions. On the one hand, it's great that they are open to adoption and want to bring more children into their family. On the other, there are hundreds of childless couples waiting to adopt.

Who will be chosen?

How are the decisions made?

I wish I knew.

The Baby Box

In November, the CGC calls and says a girl is available for adoption. Are we interested? We say "yes." They say they'll get back to us, but they're considering six other couples. There's a priority list. Due to our ages, we're low on the list.

Still, I'm so excited, I can hardly think of anything else but our girl. What will she look like, laugh like, run like?

But three weeks go by. Nothing happens.

Shogo calls the orphanage. They say the girl has been placed with another family.

"I don't know if I can take this every month," I confess. I'm not very good with uncertainty. I'm getting better, I've had to, but it's not my favorite place to be.

Shogo fares much better, or perhaps keeps his feelings more skillfully in check.

I open the *Japan Times*, read about Japan's first "baby box" in Kumamoto, Japan, the *konotori no yurikago* ("white stork's cradle"). Biological parents leave their unwanted babies there anonymously. It's monitored around the clock by nurses, and when an infant is dropped off, only minutes elapse before the hospital staff whisks the newborn away.

More a crib than a box, it's in an opening in the hospital wall. There's also a sign asking parents who drop off their babies there to contact the hospital later. In its first year of operation, seventeen infants were delivered to the "stork"—four girls and thirteen boys. Nine of them came from places other than Kumamoto, some from as far away as Okinawa or Hokkaido. Letters were left with a few of them.

One-third of the parents who brought the children in were in their twenties. Thirteen percent were in their teens, and two percent were under fifteen. The children were placed in various CGCs. Sometimes the parents came back and claimed them. The hotline received five hundred calls its first year.

Life seems so random and unfair.

But still, we soldier on.

I hold onto the glimmer of hope that coming this far in the process has given me. I hold onto my fierce vision of a family, the one I've just begun to allow myself to dream about.

The Boy

In December, the CGC calls about a waiting boy. They ask if we're interested in adopting him.

We say "yes."

They say they'll get back to us, but they don't.

We wait some more.

I ask Shogo to call them, and he does. They say they've placed the child with another family. They explain that many young couples are waiting to adopt; emphasis on the "young."

Of course, I'm happy that the children have found families, but this feels like too much to endure—the waiting, the hope, the letdown—after so many years. My fierce optimism has begun to wane.

If they rank couples by age, we're always going to be on the bottom end of that scale.

I tell Shogo that I don't want to go through this every month and that we should apply at another agency that doesn't rank according to age.

He agrees. But is there such a thing?

The private agencies are expensive and take years—often

without any guarantee of a placement after a long wait and more uncertainty.

We make a promise: we'll try to keep our heads above water and our hearts above despair.

I try to hold onto that promise, try to see the glass as half-full, but I haven't heard the child's voice for a while.

I shake out my yoga mat and go through my practice. Arms over head, gathering up the light of the sun, bringing *prana* and hope back in. Bringing in light. I find power in the Warrior Pose, stillness in balancing postures like Half-Moon. I waver but I hold my ground. I open my heart in backbends, then stretch and twist. I invert, letting my world turn upside down yet again. The blood rushes to my head, clearing my mind.

When it comes time for Corpse Pose, a posture of deep letting go into the earth, I lie down on the ground, arms out by my side, palms up in surrender, and I rest.

How deeply can I let go? How much more can I surrender?

I feel the contours of my body start to dissolve, then disappear. It's as if I am no longer a body. There is no me. There is no earth. Only a shimmering field of energy. I ride its waves.

After some time, I wiggle my fingers and toes and come out of the pose. Then I sit down to meditate. I watch my breath. And then the breath too, disappears. It's no longer me breathing. I feel myself, being breathed. The breath flows through me. I'm a conduit. A vessel for this energy, this life force, this light.

This time, instead of waiting for my child's voice to come to me, I speak directly to my child.

Hold on, I say, *we're coming.*

Hug

One day, a tall young Japanese kid comes into the yoga studio for class. It's the first time he's done yoga. He's stiff and nervous. We stretch, shake, sweat, and do partner yoga. He's reluctant to touch a stranger, so I move in and partner with him. Then I let go of his arm and encourage another student to take my place. They help each other in Cobra, supporting each other's arms as they open their chests and breathe, lifting up like snakes. His heart softens. He loosens up and laughs. They lean over each other in Child's Pose, releasing their backs. It feels good to have support and be supported. They let go more deeply into the poses, with the weight of one helping the other to release.

After class, the boy comes up, lowers his voice. He says he's having emotional problems and starts to cry. I give him a hug. He holds onto me for a long time and starts to sob like a baby. Hugging a stranger, and being emotional in this way is very unusual, especially in Japan, especially in front of the whole class. But it's a good thing that he feels comfortable enough to release, or maybe he's just so deeply distraught that he can't close the floodgates.

When he recovers enough to compose himself, he bows and thanks me, and says he'll be back. I'm sure I'll never see him again.

But it doesn't matter. I'm reminded of the Japanese proverb, *ichigo ichie.*

One time, one meeting.

In life, we come this way but once.

Perpetual Yes

On New Year's Eve we go to the temple and ring the bell 108 times for every earthly desire.

A few more telephone calls come from the CGC, telling us there's another child available and asking if we are interested, only to have no further contact.

My heart shatters a bit more with each silence.

I make Shogo call the orphanage. I insist that he tell them to stop calling us every month to ask if we are interested in a different child.

"Tell them to put a perpetual 'yes' on our file, okay? Tell them that whatever child they have available, we are interested."

"I can't do that. This is Japan. There's a procedure."

"But I can do it. I'm American."

He knows me well enough to know that resistance will be futile.

"Okay. Whatever child?" he repeats.

"Yes. Whatever child." I say firmly. I know this is our fate, our journey, our path.

There is nothing to do but trust, and let go.

The Problem

Dear Sensei:

I'm writing to you because I have a problem.

I feel mentally unstable. I'm recently separated from my husband due to my mental condition. I am violent toward myself, and toward others. I don't know what to

*do. I have done yoga a few times and it's helped me to calm
down. I want to come to your Restorative Yoga class.*

*But the main reason I am writing to you is because I
am pregnant. That is my problem.*

*I'm afraid to have this child. I'm afraid I will hurt it.
I cannot be a mother now. I cannot be a good mother. I
really don't trust myself not to hurt this child. Can I come
to your yoga class this Friday night?*

I have to read the email a few times to digest it. I wonder why
this situation has presented itself to me now, and how I should
best deal with it.

"What should I do?" I ask Shogo.

"You need to write her back," he says. "Tell her what you
think, honestly."

I take some deep breaths and hit the keyboard.

I thank her for confiding in me, tell her that pregnancy can be
a blessing, but one has to be certain. I suggest professional guidance, naming some counselors for her to talk to. I urge her to contact them. I urge her to wait a bit before making a decision about
what to do. I ask her to meditate, to connect with the soul of this
child, and talk to it before making a decision. I tell her she can
come to Restorative Yoga, if she wants. Though to be honest,
some part of me hopes she won't. I am not sure I can handle facing
her. I have to be strong.

That Friday night, though, she does come to class. Early.

It's the first time we've met, and as she fills out the registra-
tion form, she pours out her story breathlessly. Others arrive,
but she corners me and continues to speak as I take out the
props. I have to move around her, but she doesn't notice or ask
to help.

When it's time to begin, I put her and the others in the poses, encourage her to be in the breath, to focus on the breath, to send healing to her own heart and mind.

She moves in the poses, cannot stay still, but she makes it through the class.

When it's time to go, we end class in silence and keep quiet while putting away the props. I request that people stay in silence until returning home, perhaps even until the next morning.

Again, she stays behind, following me around the room as I sweep the floor, empty the trash, change the towels, wipe down the counter. She complains bitterly about being pregnant, having to make this decision. She's speaking rapidly, her hands moving quick in the air, agitated. It's as if she hasn't even done yoga for the past hour and a half.

I put up my hand.

"Chieko," I say, "I understand this is a very difficult time for you. I'm not a counselor. I think you need to see a professional. They can help you make a decision."

"But they don't understand. They don't really talk to you. They just listen."

"That's something," I say pointedly. "That's a lot, in fact."

She doesn't notice. She keeps on talking, shaking her head at the burden this child has placed on her.

At 10 p.m., half an hour after everyone else has gone, I decide I've had enough, I put my hand up, signaling her to stop. I tell her it's very difficult for me to hear her story.

"What? Why?" she asks, sounded slighted.

I tell her I've been trying to get pregnant for eight years. I tell her that I grew up in a home that was sometimes violent.

She pulls her head back, surprised. For a moment, she's silent.

Then she opens her mouth again.

"I'm sorry for you. But I'm going to get rid of it," she says, closing the door behind her as she leaves.

I stand there for a long time, broom in my hand, feeling abused and shattered.

Obsession

Something breaks in me after that.

Shogo's feeling it, too. He's not as patient as he's been in the past, though by most objective standards, the man is still a saint. I know I haven't been the easiest person to live with. I'm prone to sudden crying fits in public places, and roller-coaster rides fueled by chocolate binges—all of which Shogo generously attributes to the hormones I've been taking.

I'm an emotional wreck, but I'm still not quite ready to throw in the towel.

I go online, find stories of women who have come through their fertility struggles. Some have done eleven IVFs only to finally get pregnant naturally. Others adopt children from far-flung corners of the world like Eritrea, say they feel the child is their soul mate. Still others come to peace with being child-free, finding other ways to express their maternal instincts.

I'm obsessed, staying up until 3 a.m. combing the Internet for information and inspiration.

"Come to bed," Shogo says wearily.

"Just let me finish this one article," I say, weeping as I read about Romanian orphans and the abominable circumstances they often come from.

"You're running yourself ragged," Shogo says. "I think you need a break."

And he clearly could use a break, too. Between helping manage the yoga studio, juggling freelance writing assignments, trying to write a novel, and supporting me in a full-time fertility quest, his hands are full. He doesn't seem to be as devastated by the disappointment as I am, but perhaps that's because he's just not showing it as much.

But it's more than that, too. I feel pulled back to India, as if the land itself can help me heal in a deep and mysterious way.

It feels like a good way to explore with the question: Why do I want to be a mother anyway?

If I can't have a child, can I discover another way to experience motherhood?

I hope another pilgrimage to India will help me find out.

I hold this wish in my heart as I head back to the Motherland. It's the perfect place to search for the mother within.

Em says she'll take care of the studio, so I sign up for the "River of Sound" tour with singer Gina Sala and a group of yogis from the Pacific Northwest.

I pack my bags and say goodbye.

Shogo hugs me, exhausted. Our dog Aska has been diagnosed with leukemia. Shogo has to stay focused on her, his baby.

Maybe all the stress has gotten to her, too.

Sahasrara

SEVENTH CHAKRA

From the Sanskrit meaning "thousand-fold" or "thousand-petaled." The
seventh chakra, or crown chakra, is located at the top of the head. It is
considered the center of transcendence, the point from which the spirit
leaves the physical body for higher realms. This chakra is associated
with spirituality. It symbolizes the higher mind, cosmic intelligence,
and union with the Absolute. It governs the central nervous system,
upper skull, cerebral cortex, and skin, and revitalizes the cerebrum.
There is no element associated with this chakra.

When this chakra is balanced you are wise, understanding, spiritually
connected, blissful, unprejudiced, aware of the world and yourself, and
connected to universal life flow. You are inspiring to others—often able
to see past, present, and future.

The Middle Way

Why do all planes to India land after midnight?

I disembark in Delhi at that ungodly hour, find myself thrust into a moving crowd. I scan the faces for my driver, find him holding up a sign that says *Miss Liza*. He guides me through the mass of people milling about the airport, talking, smoking, squatting, eating, sleeping.

The road to Delhi proper is frenetic and massive, jammed with cars, bicycles, cows, and people—each one carrying a load of some kind. Delhi itself is frenetic and massive—loud, chaotic, assaulting, especially compared to the relaxed, warm beach towns of southern India where I'd taken the Ayurvedic cures before. People seem to be living and dying in front of your eyes. We step over people on the hotel's stairwell. I'm shown my room, take a cold shower, and manage to sleep under the watchful glare of a neon sign just outside my window that blinks on and off. The rusted ceiling fan has long ago given up the ghost.

I awaken the next morning and go down to the restaurant to meet Gina and the rest of the group. We're a mix of yoga teachers, healers, artists, dancers, singers. After morning curry, chai, and a round of chants such as the Gayatri mantra to bring in the light and an ode to Ganesha, the deity who removes obstacles, we're off to the holy city of Sarnath by train.

As the old Jewish saying goes: *Man makes plans and God laughs.* Our desperate dash through miles of traffic results in having to wait eight hours on the platform for the train's arrival, then another three hours for its departure. Approached by wide-eyed people in rags holding out their hands, some of our group cower in a packed shelter. Since it's a musical tour, Gina starts to sing, and others join along. Together, we sing folk songs, mantras, and sacred songs from every culture we know. Waiting travelers from Germany and Italy take out their guitars and jam along with us. Before we know it, the entire train station has joined us in song, like one of those flash mobs on YouTube. The sounds are a beautiful mix of Sanskrit and Hebrew, Arabic, and Native American invocations. Soon, even those asking for alms drop their outstretched hands and clap to the music.

We finally board the overnight train, where we're packed into individual capsule-like compartments. Our suitcases are chained to the floor so no one will steal them while we sleep. Not that anyone does—there's too much activity on board, people chatting and eating. For us Westerners, it's also a case of nerves. We've seen too many horror stories of crashes and fires and people climbing on top of the trains and breaking open windows. Better to stay awake.

Thirteen hours later we arrive in Sarnath, Uttar Pradesh, where Buddha gave his first teaching after he'd reached enlightenment in Bodhgaya. Sacred structures from many countries line the pathway to the park's center. Deer roam the grounds. I buy carrots from a vendor to feed them. In the center of the grounds is the Dhamekha Stupa, where the Buddha delivered his famous first sermon. *Dhamekha* is a way of saying Dharma Chakra, which means the "Wheel of Dharma." The wheel symbolizes *samsara*, the eternal cycles of birth and rebirth that continue due to our endless cravings and desires. I can't believe I'm walking on the same ground that the Buddha walked on before teaching what many Buddhists consider to be the first "Turning of the Wheel."

I remember the story of the five *sadhus* with whom the Buddha had been practicing austerities before he sat under the Bodhi tree and became awakened. When they saw him at the deer park, they ran away.

When the monks shunned him, the Buddha said: "Austerities confuse the mind. In the exhaustion to which they lead, one can no longer understand the ordinary things of life, much less the truth that lies beyond the senses. So I've given up extremes—luxury and asceticism. I've discovered the Middle Way."

Swayed by this wisdom—that extremes are not the answer—the five seekers became the Buddha's first disciples. Here, in a place that is neither America nor Japan, I feel myself searching for my bearings. Where is my center? Where is my middle ground? Have I become an Asian in an American Jewish body?

This is where the Buddha also gave his famous teachings on the Four Arya Truths: There is suffering; there is a cause to suffering (desire and ignorance); there is an end to suffering; and there is a path to the end of suffering (The Eightfold Path).

The Jewish culture is full of acknowledgement of suffering. I remember words of wisdom from my Jewish grandmother Molly, who said things such as "this too shall pass."

In this holiest of places, I circumnavigate the stupa with people from all over the world, many dressed ornately in ritual attire, as I consider the Four Truths. Yes, there is suffering. Yes, there is a cause. And apparently, there is an end. But where is the path to the end of suffering?

A woman in absolute rags, five children at her feet, approaches, holding a baby in her arms. Her eyes are big and round. Her face is dirty and lined with deep creases. She shakes the child at me and holds out her other hand, saying: *Food. Money. Anything. Please.*

I feel pity, anger, injustice.

She can't be more than thirty, but looks sixty.

She has six children, and can't feed any of them. I have plenty
to eat, but no one to feed.

She might die soon, leaving these kids homeless and even more
destitute than they are now. Where is the justice in that?

Where is the divine?

Where is the holy?

All I see is suffering, right here in this holy place.

And here I am, here she is, walking the path.

We cannot *not* walk the path, because the path is everywhere.

I give her all I can, but it's not nearly enough.

It will never be enough.

Varanasi

From Sarnath, we venture to Varanasi. It's the ancient city of
Shiva, the god of destruction. Shiva is the "male" element of the
universe, in constant play with the feminine Shakti, the force of
creation.

The city is rife with the energy of death. It is the home of the
ghats, flights of stairs leading down to the Ganges, where pilgrims
come to bathe, wash their clothes, perform purification rituals,
do yoga, sell bread, candy, and flowers. They also peddle beautiful offerings of flowers, spices, incense, food in palm-leaf baskets.
Locals come to get massages and shaves. Tourists come to dip in
the river, or to spread good karma by giving alms to the destitute
clustered there. We've come to study *tabla* and practice Sanskrit
for *kirtan* at a renowned music school.

On our first night, I come down with an intense fever that
leaves me sweating, hallucinating, shaking. I cannot get out of bed,
nor rest at all. All through the night I toss and turn as voices

murmur and shout from outside, from the Ganges. Are the sounds
from the women washing clothes, men bathing, people chanting?
What is real? What is unreal?

Amid the voices I hear a small voice, sharp and plaintive.

"You never honored me," it says.

"What?" I murmur, groggy.

"You never said goodbye!"

"Who is this? What do you want?" I inquire, delirious.

"Your child. Your child," the voice calls out.

"What child?" I murmur. I've never had a child.

"Your child," it insists. The voice reverberates in my brain,
drilling back through time, twenty years, making me remember.
The time I was attacked at the School for the Deaf. The bleeding
afterward. The visit to the doctor. Eating ice cream with Jake in
the car afterward. *Butterflies are free . . .*

"Now you remember," it says.

"Yes. Yes," I repeat. It's the soul of my unborn child calling to
me. The one I lost so many years ago.

Is it a hallucination, my feverish mind? Does it matter?

The voice continues unabated, crying, accusing. I murmur
apologies.

What does it want from me?

After a while, I become aware of another presence in my room.
It's my new friend Soren, a healer, who's also on our tour. Without my asking, he stays with me, wiping the beads of sweat that
pour from my forehead, placing his hands on my head and heart,
offering me reiki and healing.

I toss and turn for hours. I sweat and shiver.

"What do you want?" I ask the voice, but there is no answer.

After midnight, my fever breaks. My body is exhausted, but
my mind is somehow clear. Soren gives me a glass of water. I drink

and sit up. Though I am weak, I suddenly know what I have to do. I tell Soren, say we have to go. Now.

He nods, helps me stand up, wraps me up in shawls and helps me walk slowly downstairs. The hotel desk clerk, who's watching Bollywood movies in his half-sleep from a brown vinyl chair split down the middle, summons a *tuk-tuk*. It's two in the morning.

He guides me out onto the street and helps me up into the rickshaw, which shoots off down the pocked dirt road, careening down the narrow darkened streets, its bell ringing like that on a magic chariot. The wheels don't seem to touch the ground. The sounds around blend with the bell, and it's all music, all chaos and magic. I feel as if we're flying, like we've entered another realm in space and time. It's as if we've been transported to a liminal twilight place. Perhaps this is the *bardo*, the threshold between life and death. I feel weightless, beyond form.

We're let out at the Jalsain Ghat, where stacks of firewood are piled high for cremations. Each piece of wood has been weighed and calculated to determine the price of a cremation. Corpses shrouded in thin white gauze are carried in bamboo stretchers through the alleys onto the ghats, then placed on the pyres. An elderly man draped in white cotton is laid atop a pyre by his family. It is doused with gasoline, then set ablaze. Prayers are said by the family, who surround him. The fires crackle. Flames and ash float into the night air as his body becomes ash, bones become dust in the starlit blackness.

This ghat is one of the most auspicious places to send someone on to the netherworld. Hindus believe that to be cremated here, to have one's ashes sent into the Holy Mother, the Ganges, is the highest honor. People bring their loved ones from far and wide to begin their final journeys here. Being cremated is believed to end the cycle of suffering and lead to *moksha*, liberation from the

186 · HERE COMES THE SUN

wheel of karma. Here, death is not something hidden, something taboo. It's part of the endless Dharma Chakra cycle of birth, life, death, rebirth.

Soren and I watch quietly. As the body is engulfed, bright orange-and-red flames lick the sky. The body breaks apart and falls, glowing, into the pyre. The flames burst into the night sky in a final spectacle, reminding me of the story of the three laughing monks who traveled from town to town making others laugh. One died on the road. His final wish was to be cremated in his kimono without first washing his body. His friends complied, and when they set him afire, his body burst into fireworks he'd hidden in his clothing. He'd died the way he'd lived, making people laugh.

I've never seen a body being burned. In Japan, bodies are burned out of sight. In the Jewish tradition, bodies are not cremated but buried, sometimes in a simple pine box, an *oron*. Before burial, they're washed and dressed in white linen clothes that have been sewn by hand without buttons or zippers. These *tachrichim* have no pockets. We can't take anything with us.

I look up, notice two Japanese high school boys standing on a pier beside the river, watching. Where did they come from? Why are they there?

When the flames have died down, we turn to buy a *diya*, a flower basket candle, from a street vendor who'd been sleeping wrapped in an orange wool blanket atop his wares. I hold the candle carefully as we walk down to the Ganges. I light the wick and kneel to say a prayer for the child I lost. I set it afloat into the "Mother."

I tell him I'm sorry we couldn't be together in this life.

You're free to go, I say. *I'm so sorry I hurt you. Forgive me.*

Go, and be happy.

I release you. Release me.

You will be protected.

You cannot be harmed any more.

I say these words to the spirit, but I know that I am really saying them to myself. I think back to the Jizo statues lining the temple grounds in Shiba Park in Tokyo. I hope Jizo's loving arms reach across the world.

Shiva Puja

We stay at the river until the candle-boat floats out of sight and the sun starts to rise. I shiver in the early hours of morning, but I already feel better. I'm grateful to Soren, this man I barely know, for nurturing and protecting me. And I'm grateful to Shogo for letting me come here, trusting.

I feel exhausted but purified, somehow cleansed and renewed. Ascending the stairs at the ghat, we make our way up the small alley to find our rickshaw still there, the driver curled up asleep on the seat. Soren taps lightly on the side of the *tuk-tuk*, and the driver awakens, happy to see us as the day dawns.

My fever is gone—it's as if it never existed. We arrive back at our hotel, where breakfast is waiting. The sounds of our group chanting float up from the cafeteria as the smells of turmeric and spice waft up from the kitchen. We drink sweet, milky, frothy morning chai—elixir of the gods. We tear apart big leaves of naan and dunk them into the rich, spicy curries. I excuse myself, go back to my room and fall into a deep, heavy sleep. Later that afternoon, there's a knock at my door. We're scheduled to go back down to the ghats. I'm nervous about seeing more cremations, but Gina tells me these ghats are different. They're full of life.

Here, the waters are believed to wash away one's sins. Families bathe, women wash clothes, men dip themselves all the way down, covering their heads with the sacred waters to be purified. We roll up our pants and make our way into the water, offering beautiful flowers on floating bamboo-leaf boats and candles. The water is cold, and rather dirty, but we sing to the Mother, praising her graces, our motley voices somehow joining together in harmony.

A couple of *sadhus* sit on the stairs. They're everywhere in Varanasi. Some are holy men, some are fakes. They live in tents, or under blankets at the riverbank. They've renounced the world, have given away their material goods and aspirations. They're stripped naked except for tattered loincloths. They live nomadic lives. Their unwashed hair is matted in dreadlocks, sometimes so long it falls down to their knees. They roam the streets or do their yoga, holding a pose for months or even years. I heard a story about how one man rolled perpetually on the streets of India as his *sadhana*, his spiritual practice, and how another held Tree Pose until his limbs atrophied. Most slip under the radar of society, floating in the margins. These *sadhus* speak to us, say they're worshipers of Shiva. One calls himself Bam Bam. He motions us into his tent, which is really a blanket stretched across two sticks and stuck into the cracks in the concrete. We duck to enter, sit on the carpeted floor. He invites us to meditate. We listen to his stories, take pictures, make offerings. A fellow *sadhu* enters, colored in yellow dust. He shares his bed and his cigarettes with us. I don't smoke, but it feels right to partake, sharing a drag with the old *sadhu*. They give us blessings in words we cannot understand. We give them money.

Later that night, our guides take us to a Shiva Lingham *puja*— a purification ritual—at an underground temple down an alley in the belly of the city.

One by one, we make our way down steep steps, heads bowed.

The cave is dark, dank, and damp, lit only by two small oil lamps that flicker in an altar in the center. I hug my arms in close, make myself small enough to glide down the entry. Stalactites glisten on the ceilings. Everything's dripping, moist. We sit on the ground, which feels like a wet, earthy, primal womb. In the center of the cave stands a stone *lingham*, a phallus. It's Shiva's, rising from the earth as a symbol of virility and power, the protruding male to Shakti's inward feminine concave. The *sadhu* chants, pouring water, yoghurt, milk, leaves, red flowers, and draping red string on the *lingham*. The ladle is passed around so we can each pour and rub these offerings onto the shape. They are *prasad*—offerings to the divine male—just as the sweets were *prasad* to the divine feminine at Amma's ashram.

The red string is wrapped around the *lingham* again and again. The remainder is then tied around our wrists from one thread and cut, going from person to person. We're being connected to each other and to the energy of Shiva, the powerful force that destroys what is not necessary for growth and transformation.

Though Shogo's far away physically, I feel him close to me here in this male underworld.

I feel for him, and for other men who have gone through this particular grief. It is easy to focus on the women and our loss. But the men who have lost a child, or lost the dream of having a child, suffer too. They often hold it inside.

Tears come. I cry for Shogo, too.

I wish for him to be happy and well.

City of Seers

The next day we go by hired car to Rishikesh, the "city of those who see." It's the yoga capital of the world, made famous by the

Beatles in the sixties. Every day, thousands of yogis pass through, seeking the wisdom of the *rishi*, the yogic sages. Yoga ashrams line the Ganges. Cafes are full of Western tourists seeking salvation.

The drive is gorgeous, and sometimes harrowing. Luckily, India has a sense of humor, and we're entertained by signs along the mountain curves warning: "Better Late than Never," "Drinking Whisky, Driving Risky," "Life Is Already Short Enough, Don't Make It Shorter." Still, many cars overtake us on the hairpin turns.

Lori hands me her earphones, blasting "Psycho Killer." *Qu'est-ce que c'est?* The song blends beats, languages, and cultures, and sends me back in time to the eighties. We laugh and sing *da da da da da da da da da da*. Finally we arrive in one piece, nerves frazzled, but unscathed. We get our rooms at the ashram, drop off our things and go to practice yoga.

I go through the poses, looking out over the Ganges. Breathing in peace, breathing out peace. I stand on my head, then stand on my shoulders. I turn my world upside down, shake up everything I think I know. I open my mind up to another world, one I've not yet experienced—motherhood. Having my own family. I tap into the seventh chakra.

I don't want to come down.

At night, we cross the bridge across town to the Parmarth Niketan Ashram to attend Ganga Aarti, a sunset festival of light. People from all over the world gather to pay homage to the Great Mother here, to be bathed in the light of *bhakti*, or devotion.

Crowds swarm around a stage with loudspeakers, where *tabla* players and musicians are setting up for the night. Men anointed with *kumkum*, red sacred lines or dots on their third eyes, wear orange robes, are swathed in orange blankets. Women in white with *bindi* sparkling from their third eyes huddle together, chant-ing Vedic hymns.

A heavy copper *aarti* lamp is lit, then passed from person to person, pilgrim to pilgrim. We join in singing *bhajans*—devotional songs—and prayers offered to Gangaji and Shiva as this special light is passed among us. The lamp is waved in the crowd in the shape of OM, the sacred sound and symbol of birth, death, life, and rebirth. A giant statue of Shiva, the Destroyer, rises from the Ganges in front of us.

I hold the *aarti* lamp in my hands, recalling my mother light-ing the Sabbath candles every Friday night, closing her eyes and sweeping the light from the flame in circular motions toward her, as if to bathe herself and all of us in that light.

As I feel the warmth of the lamp, I feel that light, and my mother, and countless mothers before her who met the Sab-bath with hope and faith. I send my mother love and blessings before I pass the lamp to my neighbor, whose face is radiant in its illumination.

The lamp makes its way from person to person until everyone there has held it, held the light. Everyone's face looks softer, glow-ing in the sunset's gentle purple light beneath the larger-than-life statue of Shiva.

The sun goes down in a blaze of pink. *Bhajans* echo over the city, hundreds of voices joining as one. I'm transported to a differ-ent place, somewhere luminous and harmonious. I never want to leave. I want to keep this feeling forever.

That night, when I return to the hotel, the receptionist tells me Shogo has called from Tokyo. I'm immediately panicked. It must be something important. Has there been an earthquake? Is his father sick?

"Don't worry!" Shogo says when I call him back, alarmed. "It's good news!"

He says the orphanage has called and that we've been matched. Finally!

A little boy is waiting for a home. The CGC thinks we'd be a good fit.

I'm so stunned I cannot speak.

"Are you there? Are you interested?" Shogo asks me the same question they asked him.

"Interested? Yes! Are you kidding? Yes! Yes! Of course I'm interested!" I shout, laughing. The word doesn't even come close to describing how *interested* I am. I can hardly stop myself from running down the halls, yelling out the news.

"Okay then," he says. "I'll tell them." I can hear the joy in his voice, too.

When we hang up, I run down the halls, knocking on doors. Everyone comes out of their rooms to congratulate me.

That night, our last in India, I can barely sleep. I can't wait to get back to Japan to meet our son. Our son. Our son. I say the words over and over to myself.

On my last morning in India, my new friends surprise me with a baby shower, draping me with orange and yellow flowers and showering me with song at the banks of the Ganges.

One by one, they offer me handmade cards, flowers, toys, and children's clothes, holding them out with both hands and bowing. I bow in return, accepting their gifts.

When did they have the chance to prepare all this?

I am overcome with emotion.

Soul Star

EIGHTH CHAKRA

Some believe there is an eighth chakra, the Soul Star, or transpersonal chakra, that links the soul/spirit to matter and to its true essence. The eighth chakra takes us beyond personality-based consciousness and into higher transpersonal awareness.

It is indescribable mystery, and transcendence. It is beyond the unknown—it is the unknowable. It is the radiant power of all life in all forms in all planes.

It is union. It is yoga.

Ancestors

A week after my return from India, two social workers from the CGC come to our house.

I scurry around the kitchen, making them roasted barley tea and setting out *mochi* sweets in red lacquer plates.

Politely, they decline. Politely, we insist. On the third time, they relent and take a sip.

Custom dispensed with, they tell us what they know about the boy. He's almost two, he's healthy, he's shy with adults, but sociable with other kids. They don't know much about his birth mother, and nothing about his birth father.

"Do you have a picture?" I ask eagerly. I can't wait to see his face!

"No. No picture," they say, shaking their heads.

I look over at Shogo, puzzled.

He shrugs.

"Really?" I say.

This astounds me. There are more people in Japan with cameras than with driver's licenses. Japan is the land of the camera.

"Sorry," the social worker says, then folds her hands on her lap.

That is, apparently, that.

She shuffles her papers, her glasses slipping to her nose. Then she looks up and asks, "So, are you interested or not?"

Again, I look to Shogo for guidance. Is there some secret Japanese subtext going on? Does he have a clue what is going on?

One thing is clear. They're not messing around with this child. He's suffered enough.

The male social worker offers an explanation.

The child had been placed with another couple, but the placement fell through because the woman became pregnant with twins.

"Are you interested?" he asks again.

Again I look over at Shogo. He nods.

"We're interested," he says. His eyes say: *No picture? No problem. You told them any child.*

Now I'm done for. I can't stop the tears that are rolling down my face, and I don't even try. He takes my hand under the table, wraps his fingers in mine.

We fill out some more paperwork, then show the social workers around our house, room by room. We walk them around the neighborhood. Shogo's father comes upstairs to meet them.

He asks about the birth mother, what kind of education she has had, what kind of job. He says he's worried about the boy. What if there's a problem down the road? What if something happens? He's shooting all kinds of questions at them, and the mood turns sour.

I shoot Shogo a look. Didn't his father give us his permission and his blessing? He had to; otherwise we wouldn't have gotten this far in the process. He's agreed to the idea of the adoption, but now he's rejected the reality. I try not to panic.

Shogo frowns.

Shogo's paternal grandfather, Masakichi, had been left in his father's arms as an infant. Masakichi's father was a lumberjack in Toyama Prefecture, in Kanazawa. He was married but had a roving eye. His wife discovered her husband's affairs and took off without her six-month old son, Masakichi. No kimono-clad wife trailing ten steps behind her man, she. The husband couldn't take care of the child, so he asked a *shusenya*, a go-between or broker, to find the child a new home.

The adoptive father was a gambler—a precursor to today's yakuza gangs. His wife was a geisha. They had no children and wanted them.

Masakichi eventually became an auto-rickshaw driver—a decidedly working-class profession. The daughter of the rickshaw company's president was working at Mitsukoshi, a fancy department store in the Ginza distict, and had her sights set on a cultured man. But she hadn't found such a man, and the clock was ticking.

Her father thought Masakichi was a good man and a hard worker, and when his daughter kept coming up empty-handed on the marriage front he suggested she give him another look. Her options were dwindling. A dedicated employee would work hard to keep the company going.

So Masakichi and the daughter married and had six children. Shogo's father, Hideaki, was the eldest, and the first in his family to go to college. Determined and ambitious, he became a professor of foreign literature. He read in English, French, German, Russian, and Chinese.

He met Shogo's mother, Kyoko, through her sister, a piano teacher.

Hideaki and Kyoko had one son, Shogo, and two daughters. These kids grew up in the sixties and seventies in a working-class neighborhood in Tokyo. Their home was filled with books, many in foreign languages.

Shogo adored his grandfather Masakichi. Learning about this assortment of characters in Shogo's ancestry pleases me, makes me feel less "outside" for my difference. But now, it is clear that my upwardly mobile, professor-of-foreign-literature father-in-law feels otherwise. It's partly his fault that his son married a Westerner. (Did foreign literature make foreign countries seem that much closer, somehow?) And now that Western woman wants to adopt.

Our ancestors link us to the past. When you enter a Japanese family, you are entering into this ancient stream, for better or worse. I realize that Shogo's father is scared of the mirror this adoption holds up to his own circumstance. He wants to go forward, not back.

Is that why he's changed his mind? Despite the famous Japanese reluctance to say no, this "no" is clear, in the presence of social workers during our official home visit and under the eyes of ancestors gazing at us from photos on the family altar. He isn't ready to give up his dream of a certain kind of family. But neither am I.

My mind is reeling as the silence, the empty space, hangs between us.

I want to kick him. Why did he initially say yes? Did he think it wouldn't really happen?

"If she'd had a good situation, she wouldn't have had to give up her child," I say, finally.

Someone clears their throat.

"It's good to bring up these concerns. Better to bring them up now than have them surface later," the woman social worker interjects, voice steady and calm.

An uncomfortable silence settles around the table. I pour more tea. I look over at the social workers, who are gazing deeply into their teacups.

I glance up at the altar, invoking Masakichi's spirit. Shogo catches my look.

"You don't have to give your blessing, just don't stand in our way," Shogo says firmly, looking directly at his father.

I hold my breath, but feel like pumping my fist in the air. This could not have been an easy thing for Shogo to say, and I'm proud of him for standing his ground. What's more, he's said it in a perfectly calm way that makes it irrefutable.

I know his father is acting out of fear, and fear is natural. It's bad enough that Shogo has brought an American woman into this man's household, but now this? I also know that this fear stems from love.

In my mind, I send him the wish for happiness, the wish to be free of suffering.

And then his "no" becomes a "yes."

When the social workers leave, I hug Aska and thank her for not biting them or peeing on their feet. She wags her tail sweetly.

She's been taking chemo pills for the leukemia. Though she has her bad days, she seems almost healthy again. But the illness makes her unpredictable.

I offer incense and thanks at the altar.

I hope the ancestors are happy.

Here Comes the Sun

While we wait for the process to move forward, Shogo and I go back to work on our novel about a female ninja, which we had begun writing in West Marin. Though she's taken a back burner, I'm always happy to reconnect with my superhero alter ego, Jet Black. She traces her roots back to the Emishi, the indigenous tribes of northern Japan who fought for their homeland when the emperor's army invaded it—a story that mirrors the history of the native Americans. It was the Emishi, Shogo teaches me, who first "named" Japan. Japanese today call their country "Nippon," written in kanji as *ni-hon*:

日本

日 (*Nichi*) means "sun" and 本 (*hon*) means "origin," literally "the place where the sun rises." But these two ideograms can also be read as "Hinomoto," meaning "Land of the Rising Sun," which was the Emishi name for their kingdom in Nara.

I'm embarrassed that I'd lived in this country for six years and never knew that. Learning such an important thing now seems fitting. Maybe the sun has finally risen for me.

I go back to the altar, offer gratitude to Shogo for his strong samurai heart, and to this country for helping me make my dream come true.

I try to envision this child, this Japanese boy, this son of the land of the rising sun.

Does he like to smile and laugh? Is he quiet and shy?

Shogo says that in his dreams, he's seen an image of a kid making an "interesting face" soaking in the bathtub.

"Interesting?" I repeat. "What could that mean?"

"I don't know," he replies. "It's just what I see."

"Does he look happy?"

"Yes. Very happy."

First Meeting, 2007

The orphanage is a pink, industrial-looking concrete building in a posh section of western Tokyo, different in look and feel than the sprawling white complex we'd visited before. The emperor founded this orphanage after the war, when many children were left without families and the country struggled to rebuild.

On February 9 we walk through the big glass doors to meet our son. I'm more nervous than I was on our wedding day. I wear the garnet ring and necklace from Ruth, hoping they will bring me luck.

We're led into the entrance hall, where a giant stuffed panda is slumped over on a bench in the waiting area.

There are no kids around. It's very quiet and orderly. *Where is everyone?*

Shogo shrugs. He wonders too. We're allowed into the playground behind the main building.

Shinji is pointed out to us. He's chubby and wears a dirty blue down jacket that makes him look even bigger. His hair is cut in a rice-bowl. He has red ruddy cheeks. His pants are too big, rolled up to his ankles, and seem filthy, too. We look at him and wave. He doesn't smile. Instead, he runs the opposite direction and hides in the corner. He doesn't want to have anything to do with us.

Shogo and I exchange glances. Wordlessly, we agree. Who could blame him? He's been down this path before. Why should he trust us?

We don't chase after him. Instead, we approach the other kids in the playground and join them in the sandbox, push them on the swings, play hide-and-go-seek.

Gradually, Shinji comes closer, observing in a cautious way. His eyes are brown and the whites have small brown spots on them. I wonder if he's sick.

Soon our hour is up. He hasn't approached us once.

We go back to our car. Shogo reaches over and touches my hand. "Don't worry. It's going to be okay."

The boy is not what I imagined my child would be. I don't know exactly what I imagined, maybe some kind of joyful greet-ing, where he runs into my arms like a scene from a movie.

I'm sure I'm not the picture he had in mind for his mother, either. For one thing, I'm white. Foreign. Not Japanese.

This is not going to work, I know it. How stupid of me to think I could even try.

I try to stifle my tears, but the more I try to push them down, the more forcefully they arise. Is this grief? Is it okay to feel grief? Shouldn't I feel happy, overjoyed?

I try to express all this to Shogo.

"It's okay. Just feel what you feel," he says, squeezing my hand.

He's in it for the long run. To him, there's no Plan B. He's not uncomfortable with sadness, or with silence, or with any of it, it seems.

I vow to take a page from his book.

Home Study

A few days later, we go back to the orphanage. This time, Shinji cautiously approaches us in the lobby, hiding behind the giant stuffed panda, but then he runs away.

His caretaker, Nakata-san, a kind young woman who's been carrying Shinji on her back since he was a baby, tells us he's doing great. *Really?* I wonder. But she knows his every expression and mood. He's so happy, she assures us.

Shogo nods optimistically, but I don't see it.

Over the weeks, the visits have gone fine, but then if a day goes by and one of us doesn't come to the orphanage, we have to start from square one again. We have to rebuild the trust. It's as if on the day we don't come, his heart closes a bit more, since he doesn't want to be hurt. I know the feeling well.

Shogo and I make a decision. We're going to go to the orphanage every day for the next few months, even if just for half an hour, until he comes home with us forever.

The more we visit, the more things seem to improve.

Finally, we make a breakthrough when we ask if we can bring our dog, Aska. If Shinji's going to be our child, we reason, then he has to meet the other members of the family too.

"She's our daughter," I say to the staff.

To our surprise, the orphanage agrees to let us bring her.

The following day, we load her in the car and drive to the orphanage. We take Aska to the back alley that runs next to the grounds by the playground. The children line up at the fence, reach their hands through to pet her. As we approach, some stay back, some run away. Those who stay at the fence make a neat line. Shinji stays at the fence. He is not afraid.

Aska goes down the line of kids, sniffing their shoes. She stops at Shinji. She's been smelling his scent on us for weeks. She knows who he is. Her tail starts to wag. She makes a smile that frightens some of the children, seems strange, maybe even menacing. But Shinji's face lights up in a megawatt smile I've never seen. He loves her!

He sticks his fingers through the fence. Aska licks them. He tries to pet her through the fence. She wags her tail.

We ask the staff if we can take Shinji on a walk with Aska on the street, away from the orphanage.

Not yet.

We put her back in the car while we go inside to visit with him.

He shares a room with three other kids, two girls and one boy. The other kids jump on us and cling to us when we come in the room. We play with blocks, puzzles, toy food, and Legos.

Of the hundred kids in the orphanage, only one is available for adoption—Shinji.

The rest remain in limbo, without parents, but legally unable to be placed with families who will care for them.

Flying Bird

"Where's *wan-wan?*"

The next time we visit the orphanage, Shinji asks where our dog is.

"Her name is Aska," we say. "It means Flying Bird."

"Ahahaha." He laughs. "I want to see her."

"We'll bring her next time," I say.

The anticipation is good for Shinji, it seems. He climbs on my lap, lets me read him a picture book. Then he plays ball with Shogo, dancing and happy. He goes to the window and holds the windowsill, dropping all the way back to the floor in a backbend. He's a yogi!

"Has he always done that?" I ask the staff.

"Always," they say.

From then on, we bring Aska every visit. And each time, Shinji warms up to us a little bit more. Finally, we can take him out of the orphanage for a walk.

Since it's our first time off the orphanage grounds with Shinji, we've been asked not to bring Aska. He's disappointed, but we take him to a nearby park that has a duck pond. He loves throwing bread into the pond. There's also a Baskin-Robbins nearby. His two great loves in the same hour—animals and ice cream.

On the street, he talks to everyone. Construction workers, old ladies, teenagers.

It turns out he's not shy at all.

Oyatsu

One day at the orphanage, we're taken into a special room to feed Shinji *oyatsu*, a snack. It's really to see if he'll eat without his familiar caretakers like Nakata-san around.

The first time, he doesn't touch his food. Maybe he feels too much pressure with all eyes on him. For all I know, he's been through this before. How much does he remember? I can tell he's a very smart boy and observes everything intently.

We don't force it.

The next time we come and sit down with him to have his snack, he sips his milk. The time after that, he drinks the whole cup.

Finally, he drinks the milk and takes a bite of his cream puff, but only eats half of it. Progress! I never thought I'd be so excited about a half-eaten cream puff.

The next visit, he eats the entire pastry, practically in one swallow. Which he apparently always does. No wonder he's so chubby. Even though I'm not thrilled about him eating a sugar-filled cream puff, this is very good news. It means we'll be able to bring him to our house for a day visit, and that means he's one step closer to coming home with us.

Day Visit

I spend the week cleaning house from top to bottom as if preparing for a visit from a head of state. When the day comes to bring him home for a few hours, my happiness is dampened when I see him. There are scratches on his face and bite marks on his arms. Why?

"Did he scratch himself?" I ask, pointing at the marks.

"We don't know," the orphanage staff says.

I sigh and try not to say anything. But I have a theory—one of the girls in his room has been acting out after we leave.

"Why does he have visitors—a mommy and daddy—and I don't?" She'd asked me one day.

I didn't know how to answer. Instead, I tried to play with her, but she was moody and sad.

"Are you sure she's not available for adoption?" I'd asked.

The staff shook their heads. I'd made it harder by asking, I know.

The staff packs a rice ball and thermos for Shinji in case he won't eat at our house. They also pack towels and a change of clothes.

We take him in our car.

He's never ridden in a car before, and he's scared. On the way to our house, he notices everything, calls out the names of birds, flowers, construction cranes, trucks, buses, cars, airplanes, helicopters. He chatters nervously, pointing out everything he sees.

After having lived within the walls of an orphanage for two years, the outside world is a symphony of sounds and sights and smells.

Everything is new, scary, and exciting. Everything is possible. And for me, too, everything feels heightened somehow. I try to be more mindful, more present, even when doing everyday things like washing the dishes, combing my hair, making a meal, listening to someone talk.

I feel grateful that I can be here, be aware, or aware when I am not being aware. Suddenly, without any trigger at all, I feel so happy to have a mind unclouded by alcohol or drugs. If you cannot have awareness and clarity, you miss so much beauty, because you ARE NOT THERE.

When you are aware, there is light, there is luminosity, there is presence.

These small moments light up to make a chain of illumination. Maybe this is enlightenment—everyday enlightenment. I try to remember this as I go through my days, counting the hours until Shinji arrives for good.

And then, on March 25, we can finally bring Shinji home for an overnight.

He sleeps in the same bed with me, tossing and turning. Of course, he would be scared. There are so many new sights, sounds, smells, and in my case, even a new language. And though the pink building he's been living in is an orphanage, it's still his home. It's familiar. It's all he's ever known.

Aska sleeps at his feet.

Finally, Shinji closes his eyes.

Listening to them breathing softly together, I bask in the joy of the moment, but I don't want to get my hopes up too high yet. Anything can happen.

So we take each day as it comes.

We read to him, play with him. He eats Shogo's soba noodles, slurping them happily. He asks for seconds. He's a big eater, enjoying everything. That's a good sign, too. He's healthy.

He celebrates his second birthday at the orphanage, dressed in a suit and tie. He blows candles out on a cake. We clap and sing.

He's starting to show signs of stress when we leave. He'll need to be toilet trained soon, and it would be good to have him home so we can start the challenge.

I try to hush my impatience and amplify my trust that things will all work out. I am not sure which is harder.

Forever

On April 19, a few weeks after Shinji's second birthday, we get the green light to bring him home forever—or at least for a few months until the court renders its final judgment and he's legally part of our family.

We bring Ai-Ai, a stuffed monkey, to comfort Shinji in the car on his trip to Magome. First, we bring it into the orphanage, and he takes it and hugs it, holding it tightly in his arms. Nakata-san cries.

But she's happy, she says, waving her hand in front of her face. I can feel how hard it is for her. I don't know this then, but Shinji is the first child she has ever taken care of at the orphanage, and she's raised him as her own.

She gives us a huge bag filled with toys, clothes, books, all lovingly bought and wrapped. I am sure this is totally against orphanage regulations, but no one stops her from giving it and we graciously accept.

Shinji tries to leave Ai-Ai behind in the foyer, placing him next to the giant panda. We have to convince him he can keep the stuffed monkey: he's never had a single thing of his own and doesn't know what to do with it.

As we pull away from the orphanage, Nakata-san is still bowing and waving until we're no longer in sight.

I hadn't noticed, but I'm bowing and waving, too.

Mama–Papa–Aska–Shinji

There's a Jewish blessing for bringing home a child. Almost as soon as we get in the door, I light a candle and say the blessing. Shinji and Shogo look on, with Aska at his side and the bag of gifts on the floor.

> *May our home always be a* mikdash ma'at, *a small*
> *sanctuary filled with Your presence.*
> *May we reach out to each other in love.*
> *May our hearts be turned to one another*
> *May we create bonds of trust and care*
> *That will keep us close as we grow together as a family.*
> *Bless us, Source of Life, all of us together with the*
> *Light of Your presence.*

It's strange to have him here with us after so many years of imagining this very moment.

I think the prayer must be working.

At home, Shinji is so polite. He helps me with the dishes. He carries my bags. He follows me into the bathroom. He asks before he does anything.

"Is it okay? *Ii desu ka?* Can I eat? Can I get up from the table? *Ii desu ka?* Can I pet the dog? *Ii desu ka?*"

I know this asking for permission will soon be a thing of the past, and I savor it. It's clear he's on his best behavior. His desire to please us is so beautiful, it breaks my heart.

He hardly has to try.

Slowly but surely, my heart begins to wrap itself around this little boy.

At night in bed, after I read him a bedtime story and before he drifts off to sleep, he says, "*Mama, Papa, Aska, Shinji*" over and over, as a question,wrapping his head around this new unit, branding it into his heart.

"Mama, Papa, Aska, Shinji?" he asks.

"*Hai*," I reply. "Yes."

"Mama, Papa, Aska, Shinji?" he asks again.

"Mama, Papa, Aska, Shinji," I repeat, over and over until he falls asleep.

I think of the Yiddish expression: *A kindersher saichel iz oichet a saichel*. A child's wisdom is also wisdom.

Mama, Papa, Aska, Shinji. I need to learn this too, to brand it into my heart. It's our mantra. We are a family. We'll be together. We'll stay together.

And my father-in-law (now *Ojiichan*, or Grandpa) can't help but love him. Maybe, I think, love can be the new bloodline.

Despite the odds, the "outer" has joined this family's "inner" once again.

Ownership

We go to a playground where Shinji can see the bullet trains passing overhead. He approaches the other kids and wants to play with their toys, or play with their balls, or play with them in general. He likes to hold hands. He wants contact, touch, close-ness. Because he grew up in an orphanage where everything was communal, he misses it. He has no concept of personal ownership. Sometimes his behavior is jarring, too forward here.

At the playground, I can't say the things he does, or does not do, are "just like me" as a birth parent might do.

And this is a good thing, I decide. I have no choice but to take Shinji on his own terms. He is the way he is because that is who he is. Not because of me. Or Shogo. Maybe his gregarious playground behavior is just like his biological mother's or father's.

I'll never know.

He is his own person. I see this so clearly, how we project so much of ourselves onto our children. It's a good perspective, and it stops me in my tracks.

I can't project. Not yet anyway.

I see that at least for now, he is the opposite of other kids, who have to learn how to share. He brings his own toys to share, but the other kids don't take much interest in them. I don't want to try to make sense of things like this, or explain everything to him. He'll learn. I want to cut a path in this crazy forest of life with him.

So I practice sitting Zen. Walking Zen. Playing Zen. Mothering Zen. It's all practice, and we have a lifetime.

But my aunt Peggy doesn't. She sends an email, says her cancer has spread and she's in great pain.

She's about to go into hospice. She doesn't have much time left.

She wants to meet Shinji before she dies.

CALIFORNIA
_____

All That Has Divided Us Will Merge

Though there are many customs for birth in Japan—the mother returning to her parents' house, a celebration of the child's first solid foods—we'd missed them all. So when we return to California, my mother decides to hold a Jewish baby-naming ceremony for Shinji.

Many people from her community gather to welcome him, though we are strangers. Shinji is given the name Benjamin—his middle name.

In the Jewish tradition, it is customary to throw breadcrumbs into a body of water as a symbolic act of repentance, any time between Rosh Hashanah and Yom Kippur. The ritual is called Tashlich, a Sending Out. We gather along the Napa River to "cast away" the sins of the past and resolve that next year will be a better one.

My mother and stepfather, my father and stepmother, my sisters and their sons are there. Peggy is too sick to join us, and I feel her absence on a day when the whole family has gathered to heal and rejoice. The past is behind us, the future is wide open. It's a time of new beginnings, a holy time all over the world. In India it is the Ganesha Festival, honoring the Elephant God of new beginnings and remover of obstacles. In the Muslim world, it is Ramadan.

My mother's friends come up to congratulate us. Some tell me their stories, of how they too were adopted, or how they have adopted children, and what a wonderful *mitzvah*, good deed, it is. I agree, thinking it is Shinji's *mitzvah* to us.

Tossing bread into the water, everything is still. It is a beautiful moment.

The congregation has prepared a special blessing. It says:

> *May the one who blessed your ancestors bless you. We*
> *hope that you will be a blessing to everyone you know,*
> *humanity is blessed to have you.*

Shinji sits atop Shogo's shoulders wearing his beaded *yarmulke*, smiling and dancing. I look at Shogo and see that he is crying, too.

The adults gather and say the Shabbat prayer:

> *And then all that has divided us will merge*
> *Then compassion will be wedded to power*
> *And then softness will come to a world that is harsh*
> *and unkind*
> *And then both women and men will be gentle*
> *And then both men and women will be strong*
> *And then no person will be subject to another's will*
> *And then all will be rich and free and varied*
> *And then the greed of some will give way to the needs*
> *of many*
> *Then all will share equally in the Earth's abundance*
> *And then all will care for the sick and the weak and*
> *the old*
> *And then all will nourish the young*
> *And then all will cherish life's creatures*
> *And then all will live in harmony with each other and*
> *the environment*
> *And then everywhere will be called Eden once again.*

My mother has ordered a special cake for Shinji decorated with Pokémon, though Shinji seems to be the only one there who does not know who Pokémon is. He devours the cake, which says: "*Mazel Tov*, Shinji. Welcome to the Tribe."

Wisdom

After the baby naming, we drive down to Half Moon Bay. Peggy and her husband have bought Shinji a giant purple, spotted T-Rex. Shinji holds it on his lap as Peggy holds him on her lap.

He refuses to put on his diapers, so I ask him to put them on the dinosaur instead. This he agrees to. He gives a demonstration to Peggy, teaching her and the dinosaur how to wear the diapers properly. Then he chases Peggy's cats Rosie and Reba, who hide under the beds. He's determined to pick them up, to hold them. Eventually, he wins them over by dangling their mouse toy and proffering treats.

We walk down a path toward the beach. A homeless man with a cat is camped out on the path. The cat has been hit by a car, the man needs money for its hospital bills. Others walk by the man and the cat, but Shinji pulls my arm, insists on stopping to pet the cat. Then he sits down on the path and tries to pick the cat up, to hug it. I tell him the cat is hurt and he shouldn't touch it. So he pets it instead. People stop to look at the little boy sitting on the path, blocking their way. A mother pulls her children away. A photographer stops to take a picture. Others start to put money in the basket. More children come to sit by Shinji's side.

Somehow, he brings together the splintered worlds of strangers.

"He's so beautiful," Peggy says.

"I think so, too. We're so lucky."

She takes my hand. I feel her pulse, like the little heart of a bird, beating in my palm. I don't want her to die.

The next day, Shogo has to go back to Japan. He takes Shinji with him.

I stay in California for another week alone, knowing it might be my last time to be with her.

We go to yoga together, and Peggy amazes me by kicking up into Forearm Stand at the wall, even though she barely weighs ninety pounds.

"I'm not going down without a fight," she says.

We walk down to the beach, the cool ocean breeze hitting our faces. Peggy takes her time, putting one foot in front of the other as each step sinks into the sand. I slow down to match her pace.

We walk in silence. No cars, no horns, no cell phones, no trains, no sirens, only the sound of the ocean, rolling in, rolling out. Only the sound of the surf and her labored breath.

It's hard to see her struggling, weak. She'd always been vibrant, dynamic, full of life and energy. She doesn't want to die, she says, and I've done everything I can to help ease her mind. My friend Master Li gives her weekly Qigong sessions, and she revives to the extent that the doctors can't believe she's got fourth-stage pancreatic cancer.

But she does.

On her down days, she's prepared for the worst. She calls her life-long friends, inviting them over to sit with her in her walk-in closet. She pulls out her favorite outfits, makes us all try them on like we're at a fashion show.

"I think you'd look great in the purple Marni sweater," she says to Stephanie. To me, she gives a black cashmere coat from Barney's. She's never spent money on jewelry, so there's nothing to pass on there. Fashion has always been her love. Stacks of *W* and *Vogue* were always piled up on her coffee table, mixed in with *Ms.* and *Mother Jones*.

The whole time I stay with her, I wear the coat—at her insistence. I am ridiculously overdressed for a beach walk. Up ahead, a Golden Retriever rolls around on the sand. Something must have died and he's rubbing the scent onto his coat.

As we approach the dog, I see a mottled gray disk in the sand. I'm careful to lift up the bottom of the coat as I bend down in the sand to pick up the round orb. Two prongs stick out from it. It's porous, like washed stone.

I hand it to Peggy, a question in my eyes.

"It's the vertebra of a whale. They sometimes wash up here," she says.

"Hmmmh. All that's left of an eight-thousand-pound creature. This little half-pound bone."

I nod, turning it over in my palm. The essence of the whale is still in it, somewhere. In the bone and the marrow.

"In two hundred years, all those houses could be gone," Peggy says, looking up at the small village.

I'm not sure if she takes comfort from this fact, or if it worries her.

"Everything changes," I agree.

"I'm proud of you for persevering."

"I'm still worried that something might happen, that it could all fall through."

Now that Shinji has come home, we have to foster him for a while. Then we will have a court date to hear the judge's decision as to whether or not we can keep him. Between now and then, his birth mother could resurface and change her mind.

"Things can change in an instant."

"They can," she says. "But if it's meant to be, it will be. He will be yours and you will be his. *Beshert.*"

"I hope so," I say.

"It's the one regret I had. I'm glad you moved forward with it."

"Because of you." I say.

I swallow back tears.

I try not to latch onto the fact that we might finally have a child but that my aunt won't be around to get to know him. Still, she's met him, and that is what matters.

We walk slowly, hand in hand, back to her dream house. It, too, will be gone someday.

I hug the coat closer. I inhale her perfume, tinged with salt water in the sea-soaked air. I know she's put her wisdom on me like an animal spreading its scent to protect its child.

I'll keep it as long as I live.

"I wish I didn't have to go," she says.

"Me too," I say, grateful she hasn't used the word "die."

I don't want to use it, either. I don't want to believe in death. I want to believe in somewhere beyond time, something like the ocean itself, which empties out and fills up, over and over again. I want to believe that we are infinite and limitless, beyond time and space, connected to source, to that which never dies and is never born. I want to believe that we will meet again.

JAPAN

Skinship

Back in Japan, I spend extra time with Shinji, trying to make up for the time I've been away in California. I take him to the park, the zoo, and the local *sento*. There aren't many bathhouses left in Tokyo, but a few can still be found. Our neighborhood has a good one with special mineral baths. People come from all over to soak in its healing waters. Some of the bathers are in their nineties and have been coming their whole lives.

I love the therapy, the purification. I love the deliciously hot tubs and the sense of community that makes the *sento* a rare encounter with a local way of life.

Men and women bathed together until the Meiji period, when modern reforms placed a wall between them, with a *noren* curtain indicating male and female and separating the sides. Now kids of the opposite sex can bathe with their mothers until elementary school. Then they're on their own.

I love the *hekiga* mural, of gaudy Mt. Fuji, and the outdoor *getabako* shoe shelf, named after the traditional wooden slatted shoe—*geta*. And I love the ritual. As with every activity in Japan, there's a special way to *sento* bathing. Specific steps ingrained in childhood.

I know the drill, and I'm happy to be able to teach it to Shinji. It might be one of the first—and last—cultural lessons that a Western mother can teach her Japanese child.

First you take off your shoes, put them in the box. You take your shoebox key into the changing room, where you get a locker with another key. You put your clothes in the locker and go into the baths naked. Sometimes there is a small towel to hold out in front of you for modesty, though if you are the size of most foreigners, it is purely for show.

In the baths, you take a stool and place your bucket in front of a faucet, securing your own station. A thin body-scrubbing towel is a necessity as you must lather every inch of skin, rinsing several times before entering the baths. Signs show red-faced bathers breaking the rules, warning: *No soap in the tubs! No soap residue on the skin! No washing clothes! No tattoos! No swimming!*

The younger generations scrub the older; friends and family members scrub each other. Then they repeat the ritual. There's a Japanese expression for the closeness one feels when bathing: *hadaka no tsukiai,* or "skinship." When I went to my local *sento* for the first time, I was scared I'd be turned away. I wasn't. Now I'm a regular. I've never been so clean in my life.

A group of women bathe there daily. One brings fresh fruit to share. We talk about work, family, the neighborhood. I've been talking about Shinji for months. These women finally get to meet him, to welcome him into the community. The women take turns holding him, and he doesn't wiggle away.

"He's so handsome," they say, and they're right. He's unrecognizable as the chubby little boy in dirty clothes I first met. He's slimmed down due to the healthy brown rice, fish, and vegetable meals Shogo cooks. Those mysterious spots on his eyes are gone. His skin is shiny and healthy. And he's happy.

I've only got a few years left to enjoy this special time with Shinji. Soon it will be gone, as he'll be too old to bathe with the women, and will join the men.

I sit in front of the mirror and scrub Shinji's back. Then I turn around to do mine; but for the first time ever, a friend pulls up her stool and offers to scrub my back. As she swirls the soapy cloth around my spine and shoulders, I feel the tension drop away.

Two decades, two continents, and two thousand Sun Salutations later, I finally feel at home.

Shinji and I soak in the hot mineral bath, then jump into the cold plunge. Shinji loves the ice-cold soaking pool. He swims like a fish, slapping the water excitedly.

I let myself sink deep into the water. I revel in the freedom we women have, at home in our bodies.

I soap myself up, massaging my heart and my womb. I circle the washcloth with love and appreciation. Imperfect though my body may be, it is perfect for me.

Butterfly

In March, an investigator comes over to tell us that Shinji's birth mother did not show up for her court date. Despite repeated attempts, she has not been located, so the court date to finalize the adoption will proceed as planned.

One month later, Peggy passes away.

I'm stricken with grief. Just before she died, she sent packages full of books, toys, and clothes for Shinji, even a Tibetan lantern that turned, reflecting the wheel of birth-life-death-rebirth. She was a Bodhisattva, thinking of others even as she herself lay dying.

I fly back to California for the memorial. Two hundred people come to celebrate her life—people from every walk of life—Rastas in waist-long dreadlocks, dykes on bikes in flannel, grandmas with purple hair, grandpas in red hats, barefoot children—the children of the children she had helped through her work. The

Rabbi is a transvestite. Buddhist monks also officiate. There's food, music, and dancing. Spontaneous tributes and drumming erupt. Her friends bring potluck dishes in Fiestaware, her favorite dishes we used to scour flea markets for when I was a teenager. Though I didn't know it then, Peggy's love of all things vintage was an American version of the Japanese aesthetic of *wabi-sabi*, a reverence for all things imperfect, incomplete, and impermanent.

I'm grateful that she inspired us to adopt Shinji, and that she got to meet him.

In the Jewish tradition, one sits *shivah* with the deceased's family for a week after the loved one has passed, offering solace and comfort. I must return to Japan, so I follow the Buddhist tradition, in which one prays for the liberation of the deceased's spirit for forty-nine days. The first twenty-one days are especially important, as that is when the soul travels to the afterlife.

For twenty-one days, I hold Peggy in my heart. Mixing traditions in Tokyo, I adopt the Jewish custom of *keriah*, tearing a garment to symbolize the rending that has occurred when the loved one has been ripped away. I tear a soft black cotton shirt Peggy gave me into pieces and wear the torn garment under my clothes. I want to keep her close to me, under my skin.

On the twenty-second day, I tell myself I simply must stop. I cannot cry forever.

Shinji has been given a pogo stick and wants to bounce on the sidewalk outside. It's dangerous, and he's a bit young for it, but he can't be stopped. He seems impervious to pain, though I know he is not. It's just that he learned not to cry at the orphanage, where help might not have been as quick and as plentiful as in other settings.

Suddenly, he points to the pavement. "*Cho cho! Cho cho!*"

A butterfly lies on the ground. A beautiful orange and black monarch.

"*Nete imasu.*" It's sleeping. I use the Japanese euphemism for death.

He leans over its lifeless body. "*Shinda?*" he asks. Is it dead?

I wonder how, and where, he has learned that word.

"Yes," I say, scooping up the butterfly in my hands and bringing it over to the garbage. But this will not do.

"*Hana! Hana!*" He stomps his feet and motions to a potted daisy bush in front of the house. Understanding, I carry the butterfly over and put it to rest on the bed of flowers. He covers it with a leaf.

Then he points up. *Sora*, he says. Sky. Satisfied, he takes my hand and leads me back to the pogo stick, where he bounces and bounces until dinnertime.

* * *

I'm devastated by Peggy's death, but Shinji's arrival has given me a sense of contentment and renewal. Still, I'm wary of growing complacent. Something could still change before the adoption is finalized.

In the weeks and months to come, I try not to think about what could go wrong. Instead, I focus on all the little miracles. Shinji has adjusted well to home life, eats up a storm, sleeps soundly through the night.

Finally, our court date to finalize the adoption arrives. We get dressed for our interview—Shogo and Shinji in suits and ties, me in a black skirt, white silk blouse, and high heels.

Shogo clasps the garnet necklace around my neck.

I close my eyes, touch it for a moment, as if it is a sacred amulet. Which to me, now, it is. What else could a "sacred amulet" be than this? Something which connects us to our own wishes and dreams, inspiring and empowering us to manifest them?

We take the train to the Imperial Palace grounds at Hibiya Park, walk halfway around the moat to the courthouse.

The sun is shining brightly, and the day is clear.

Once inside the building, we give our names, and wait. Each minute seems endless, like a year. I try to be patient. This is it. The last step. The end of the long, long road. What's twenty more minutes after a decade of waiting?

After what seems like forever, the judge finally calls us into his chambers. Shinji stands between us, tiny, looking up at the lectern where the judge presides.

He peers over his glasses halfway down his nose. In a kind voice, he says hello to Shinji. Then he asks us how it is going.

We tell him we're all happy. It's going well.

The judge asks us a few questions about parenting Shinji.

Does he eat? Sleep? Is he playful? Communicative?

We say "yes" to everything. Then we tell him that we want to keep Shinji's name, which was given to him by his mother at birth, but change the kanji for "Shinji" from

新治

which means "newly govern" to

信仁

The name will sound the same, but the characters used to write the name will be different, with different meanings.

信 (*Shin*)

means "belief" and

仁 (*Ji*)

means "kindness" or "love."

Kindness was considered the highest virtue in ancient Chinese philosophy, like Agape in Greek. So the name means, literally, "belief in kindness."

The judge agrees to the name change. He asks us how we'll educate our boy in the future. We say we will do whatever it takes, whatever works. Shinji seems comfortable in Japanese kindergarten, so that's where he'll go. Maybe later he'll go to an international school. It's harder for me to keep him in Japanese schools, where the curriculum and customs are foreign to me, but since he's Japanese, it is better for him. I'll adapt. If things change down the line, we'll reconsider.

The judge declares the adoption final and issues our adoption decree. He brings his gavel down on the documents, his stamp of approval complete. He leans over and congratulates us. We are now family.

It's official.

We leave the chambers and walk around the palace moat.

Finally, I can breathe a sigh of relief.

But I can't exhale completely, because once the judge renders a decision on an adoption, the court must wait another two weeks to give the birth mother or interested third parties a chance to make any last pleas.

This is because we've applied for a "special" adoption, since Shinji's birth mother cannot be located. By law, the social workers must try to find her before the adoption is finalized and notify her of the impending decision.

As we walk back toward the subway station, I recall jogging along this very path when Shogo and I first started going out.

Before we were a couple. Before we were a family.

This old palace path hasn't changed. But it has, because now Shinji holds each of our hands as we walk along it, swinging between us.

We take Shinji out for ramen, his favorite food. We raise our *oolong-cha* glasses in a cheer of *kanpai!*

"*L'chaim*," Shinji says with a big smile on his face.

This is a Hebrew word he's heard from Grandma in California. Somehow, it's stuck.

"To life," Shogo says as we clink our glasses together.

"To life," I reply.

"Why are you crying, Mommy?" Shinji asks.

I never thought I'd live to see the day someone called me Mommy.

He asks again.

"Because I'm happy," I reply

He turns to me and smiles.

"Then you should be laughing," he says.

And then, just like that, I am.

Dyeing a Cloth

My friend Ted, who'd lost his young son, posts an elegy on his blog. It's a beautiful picture of his boy in front of a drum set, smiling broadly, drumsticks raised in the air. No words.

I send Ted an email.

He writes back, tells me that the mother of his son has moved to Southeast Asia, where she's working at an orphanage. She wants to help other children.

Ted is planning the next step in his own life.

"Let me know what I can do to help," I write.

I've come to think that motherhood is a practice, a lot like meditation. And meditation, my mantra teacher Gina once said, is a lot like dyeing a cloth red. You take a cloth and dye it red. The sun bleaches it white so you dye it again. The sun bleaches it white again, and you dye it red again, over and over.

In spiritual terms, you do this many times. You keep doing it until it becomes habit, until the color sticks.

Which means, you don't try to push away the pain. And you don't get too attached to the joy, either. You just try to experience it all as fully as you can, knowing that everything changes.

I admire this about Ted. He seems to sit with the pain. And when you sit with it, it begins to lose some of its power. Then joy can somehow more easily arise. And then you feel the joy even more than before.

Though it is new to me, this understanding is nothing new. In the "Third Turning of the Wheel" in the ancient Buddhist Yogacara tradition, the process is to embrace the uncomfortable feelings of suffering we want to push away, to view these things as not "outside" ourselves.

Through "emptiness" or *shunyata*, which we enter through meditation, we realize that everything we're perceiving is a quality and concept that is not separate from us, the perceiver.

Seeing things as outside of ourselves is an "incorrect view." According to this tradition, it is *all* arising from our own minds. This "Third Turning of the Wheel" is the understanding of dependent arising, or a "non-dual" view.

Dualism means that the mind rests in opposites, such as attraction or aversion, and thinks they're real. This creates separation from ourselves and our experience. But when the mind goes beyond opposites, beyond concepts, we can enter "big mind," or universal consciousness, or non-dualism. This is called the clear light, the god-realm, the divine, grace, or whatever we want to label it.

When we realize that all the labels are coming from us—indeed everything we see and experience is coming from us—we can awaken Buddha mind, discover our essential Buddha nature, and abide in the infinite place where self and world, mind and matter, mother and child, death and life are all one.

Bearing this in mind, I try to make it my practice to try to see everything as miraculous and divine—the sacred and the profane—the triumphs and the struggles.

And, at the very least, if I can't help people, I vow to try to stop hurting them—in thought, word, and deed.

I try not to think about the possibility of Shinji's mother making a plea to reclaim him in these final two weeks. More than anything, I wish that she won't, but if she does, who am I to prevent their reunion?

Thoughts like these send me into a tailspin. I wish his mother well, but I can't bear the thought of Shinji being taken away from us at this stage.

I take refuge in my yoga mat, notice my mind and how it labels what I experience. In a yoga pose, aside from extreme discomfort or injurious pain, you could label a response "uncomfortable" or you could experience the energetics of *ki* moving in the body as "pleasurable." Or, you could take away the idea or label of "discomfort" or "pain" and just experience the sensations—just being present with whatever arises.

You can re-label a sensation and change its effect.

I try to notice the labels I attach to what I experience, and see if I can change them. It's hard to do this in yoga, but way harder off the mat in life.

The weeks are agony for me, though Shogo remains calm and optimistic.

Finally, the date comes and goes. No contact has been made.

We're free and clear. But what of Shinji?

If he wants to find his birth mother someday in the future, will he hit the same walls? How will that make him feel? How will he be able to live with that?

Will he see the wall as a possibility for growth?

I go back to my meditation cushion and sit.

I send Shinji and his birth mother the wish for happiness, to be free of pain, to be at peace.

Mata

Daphne, whom I last saw in India, comes to Tokyo with her angelic voice and guitar to give a concert. She sings hymns to the mother from her CD, *Mata*. It's been three years since our visit to Amma's ashram. Fifty people gather in the small space of Sun and Moon, mostly women. Daphne encourages us to open our hearts and sing to our mothers, to the mothers within us. I'm surprised when Chieko walks in and comes to sit down across from me. I haven't seen her since her email about her pregnancy, after which she came to class and told me about her *mizuko*.

Daphne's voice is strong and vulnerable, full of beauty and femininity. We rock against each other, swaying to the music. In the middle of the song, Shinji, who's been wandering amidst people at the gathering, comes and sits on my lap. I bend down to inhale the sweet baby-like smell of his hair. My precious child.

When I look up, Chieko is looking at us, crying. I try to stay with the lyrics, but my heart is telling me to *do* something. I'm her teacher. I'm supposed to be bigger than the past, bigger than my hurts and pains. I've been teaching my students to transcend and include. What am I waiting for myself?

"Screw it," I say, getting up and balancing Shinji on my hip as I go sit beside her.

As the music continues and the chanting grows louder, I lean into her a bit, let her lean into me.

I inch my hand toward hers, chanting *mata, mata, mata*.

She takes my hand.

Breastfeeding

A friend from California comes to visit with her six-month-old girl. She's breastfeeding. Shinji stares, transfixed. Though he's almost three now, he's never seen a woman breastfeeding. Japanese women breastfeed in private, or they cover themselves and their babies with a fabric tent to be discreet.

He pulls at my shirt, tries to get at my breast.

"Not here," I say, embarrassed. There are strangers in the room.

But he keeps pulling.

"Okay, Okay. Wait." I gather him up and take him into another room. "Do you really want to do this?" I ask.

"Yes," he replies.

I look him straight in the eye.

"You know, don't you, that nothing is going to come out, right?"

"Yeah," he says, but I'm not sure he really understands.

He pulls my breast out and climbs onto my lap.

I cradle him as he takes it in his mouth and sucks. I'm crying, trying to wipe away the tears. After a while, he looks up at me and says, "It's delicious."

All that season, he pulls at my shirt. And all that season, I give him my breast when he wants it.

We both know nothing comes out, but I want him to have the experience of being at his mother's breast, however inadequate it might be.

I've heard stories of adoptive mothers inducing lactation, but it's too late for that for me. Besides which, it seems that for now, imagination is enough.

By the time the summer is over, he no longer pulls on my shirt.

Names

In the fall, we go back to court to ask for approval to give Shinji a middle name. We want to give him a Western name, so he can have some connection to me and to my culture.

Middle names are virtually unheard of in Japan, unlike in

English-speaking countries, where they've been used since the late seventeenth century. Surnames didn't appear in Japan until the mid-nineteenth century. Before then, commoners could use the name of a birthplace or a physical attribute of their homeland as a family name. In Shogo's case, Oketani means "barrel in the valley." Perhaps sake or vinegar was made in his ancestral home.

Japanese *koseki* family registries (equivalent to Western marriage and birth certificates) have no place for middle names. If we were to add one, there wouldn't be a place for it in my husband's family registry—nor on our son's passport, school records, insurance papers, and other official documents. Once again, would carving out such a place be worth the trouble?

My middle name meant something to me. Sharing a name with my heroine, Anne Frank, had connected me to something larger than myself. This is what I'm thinking of now.

"It will be difficult for him in school," the judge cautions. "He might be teased."

"Maybe. But he'll have American nationality, too, so it's good to have an American name," Shogo says.

The judge agrees. We tell him we're already informally using Benjamin, after my maternal grandfather, a metalworker from Ludz, Poland, and also after Walter Benjamin, the writer/Resistance fighter Shogo and I talked about so many years ago.

The judge pounds his stamp on the papers and rules us legal. Shinji gets his shining middle name.

Soon, Shinji's middle name is entered into our *koseki*.

But as usual, there isn't enough space.

But by now, the clerks at the ward office expect our special requests. Some things have changed over the past two decades, and somehow they manage to roll with it.

And something else has changed, too. I put Shinji to bed later that night, and then I sit down to meditate. When I first began to meditate, I sat to escape from pain. Now, when I sit, I realize that I'm not running away from anything.

I sit to abide in gratitude and peace.

Kindergarten

Shinji starts kindergarten at three years old, younger than in America. It's really too late to apply, and there are waiting lists and all manner of competition at the nearby private school, but Shogo's aunt is the piano teacher at a private kindergarten and we get in.

Before school starts, we take him to the grounds and introduce him to all the teachers, let him play in the playground. The bus that will take him to and from school is painted like a turtle, in bright yellows and greens, with a tail on the rear, near the lights. It's a play on the school's name, Kameda Kindergarten. *Kame* means turtle.

We tell him how wonderful it's going to be for him to ride the bus. He can't wait.

He's outfitted in a navy blue uniform that makes him look like a mini-sailor, with a hat and blue knee-length socks and a special backpack and *uwabaki*, special white shoes just to wear indoors.

There are all sorts of accouterments to bring, and they all have to be sewn to specific sizes and specifications. There are pages and pages of notes and instructions.

Shogo's sister Ayano, herself a school teacher, comes to the rescue by sewing the lunch mats and pencil cases and towel bags and all manner of things I don't even know he needs until she's already made them.

Shogo has worked at home for half a year while Shinji acclimates, but is happy to go back to an office. He gets up early to make Shinji's *bento* boxes, then goes to work as an editor at a publishing house.

The first day of school, the parents attend the opening ceremony. It's a big deal, and everyone dresses up. Shogo wears a navy suit and pressed white shirt, black loafers, and Armani tie. I wear Peggy's black one-piece Max Mara dress, her vintage cashmere sweater, and pearls from my mother.

When it comes time for the kids to separate from their parents, Shinji cries and cries. He clings on to me and has to be dragged out into the other room.

"He's not like the other kids," I start to say. "He has separation anxiety, he's only been with us for . . ."

But the headmistress shoots me a look. "He'll be fine," she says.

I stammer and reach for him. She spirits him away.

And sure enough, he is fine.

It's me who's the wreck, like my stepmother Nancy was that day Shogo first met her, when Shogo delivered the infamous sake barrel and my half-sister went off to kindergarten.

Kids leave. They slay dragons. And that's how it should be.

From then on, Shinji takes the fifteen-minute bus ride to school every day. We take Aska down to the bus stop and put Shinji on, waving until he's out of sight.

He makes friends and enjoys the school, which specializes in music.

Although I worried about having him in Japanese schools, he is Japanese, after all. He'd be uncomfortable in an international school even though it would make my life easier—if we could afford it. Which we can't.

So for now, as we told the judge, we'll leave him in Japanese schools, where he feels at home and where the other mothers seem to accept me for who I am.

Nowhere is the dreaded competition or the "new mother wars" I've heard so much about. Things like women snubbing each other over less-than-artful *bento* lunches or turning a cold shoulder to the newbies on the PTA.

I don't see anything like this, until I take him to the park.

And then, it's not the mothers, but the other kids who take him to task.

Nanijin?

At the park, other kids look at him, then look up at me, then back at him, trying to figure us out. I'm white, foreign. He's Asian, dark. We're a rare sight. I speak to him in English. He answers me in Japanese.

The kids ask questions. "*Nanijin?*" What kind of person are you?

"*Uchujin*," he replies. I'm an alien.

We laugh, but the other kids aren't amused. They want a real answer.

"*Nihonjin? Amerikajin?*" Japanese? American?

"*Dochira deshoo . . .*" he replies ambigously. I wonder which.

"*Hafu? Double?*" Are you half? Are you whole? They press their case.

"What are you?" He turns the question around to them.

They turn and run away.

In the past, episodes like this make me wonder why I stay here, but now I know. Because the walls I hit make me grow. I hope the same will be true for Shinji. After all, he doesn't have a choice but to be who he is. To stand out in a country where standing out is difficult, if not sometimes impossible. Yet, in some sense he has chosen us, as we have chosen him.

We go to a Passover Seder at a friend's house. Explaining the objects on the Seder plate to Shogo and Shinji, I reclaim my own traditions. All the foods—*maror* (bitter herb), *charoset* (fruit and nut paste)—are symbolic of some aspect of slavery, as Jews had once been slaves, too.

We taste these foods to honor our ancestors and to remember our roots, so we might better appreciate life's sweetness, so that we can savor our freedoms.

From My Heart

Shinji tells me that the mother of one of his classmates is pregnant, her belly round and full. He looks sad, confused.

I come to sit beside him.

He asks, "Did I come from your belly?"

I put my arm around him, consider how to answer.

What did Dietmar say? I wrack my brain, trying to remember.

"No, you came from my heart," I reply.

He nods, mulling it over. He's five years old now. Does he understand?

He buries his head in the couch and cries.

"What are you feeling?" I ask, patting his back.

He doesn't answer, just continues to cry. It's the first time since he's been with us that he's cried spontaneously—not because he's wanted something he hasn't gotten, or is physically hurt, or frustrated.

I sit with him for awhile. Because of the yoga and meditation, I can just sit with his pain and my discomfort. I don't try to push it away, analyze, it or even process it, really.

I just let myself feel the sadness, the pain that he feels.

I know that my job is not to fix him or try to heal him. It's to be present with him, to honor his experience, to give him the space to be as he is, and to hopefully heal himself.

"I was all alone," he says after a while.

"When?

"Then."

"At the orphanage?" I prompt.

"Yes."

"How did you feel then?"

"I felt lonely."

"That must have been really hard," I say.

He nods, continues to cry.

"Even though you might have felt alone, you weren't really alone, right? Nakata-san was there."

"Hmm," he says, considering.

"She took care of you. And your friends were there."

He stops crying.

"Can I see the album?" he says later, when Shogo comes home from work.

I take it out. We sit on the couch together, flipping through the pictures of him at the orphanage, dressed up in a little suit and tie on his birthday, or with a ninja headband at the orphanage athletic meet. There are pictures of him at the dusty playground where we first met him, in the playroom full of toys.

"Where are mommy and daddy?" Shinji asks.

I look at Shogo. I'm not sure what to say.

Shogo says, "We're taking the pictures."

Shinji *humphs*, but seems satisfied.

Later, after he's gone to bed, I ask Shogo why he said that. He explains that it's enough for Shinji to see the orphanage, to wrap his head around it, to process that much for now.

"He'll figure it out, and we can tell him little by little, right?"

House of Dreams

With Shogo at work and Shinji off to kindergarten, I decide that it's time to start writing. I take a pillow, notebook, and pen—a laptop seems a travesty in such a place—and crouch down to enter the teahouse. I sit on the *tatami* and wait, but nothing comes.

Without the ring of the telephone, the doorbell, or email, the teahouse is too quiet. I can't seem to write. So I do what I always do—procrastinate. I sweep the *tatami*, I dust the walls, I light incense, put flowers on the altar.

Then I sit back down and face the blank page. Again.

And still, I write nothing. Not a Zen nothing—a real nothing.

I shiver from the cold. There's very little difference between being outside and in, but hadn't I romanticized that fact about this place, this sanctuary my mother-in-law had loved so dearly?

A century earlier, Thoreau—who'd lived in a hut in the woods—wrote: "A man is rich in proportion to the number of things which he can afford to let alone." With a teahouse in Tokyo, I felt as if I'd struck gold. And there was much I wanted to "let alone."

I'd always blamed my inability to write on lack of time, space, and quiet. Now that I have all three, what was there to blame?

I close my eyes, take some deep breaths, try to drop into a meditative state.

And then I start to hear things, as Shogo's mother did. Frogs croaking. Wind rattling against the windows. Leaves falling ever so softly onto the roof. What I've mistaken for "silence" is really a symphony.

I understand that this thing—The House of Dreams—is a construct. A little hut built by humans for worldly enjoyment. Nature was there first, with its own cacophony and chaos. The original inhabitants of this garden have arranged their lives around this quaint obstruction.

I need to be like Issa, the old haiku master, who wrote:

> *Spiders, never fear—*
> *I keep house*
> *casually.*

Humbled, I notice the different strains of the frog's song, the unique designs of each spider's web. I want to take a page from how Issa observed the world in this small universe, which expanded his own.

> *Every creeping thing,*
> *Listen!*
> *The bell of impermanence.*

As I track the comings and goings of my tiny roommates with reverence, I know I'm not alone. And I know I don't have forever. Not with that bell of impermanence ringing.

And so I write a letter to Nakata-san, Shinji's caretaker at the orphanage.

In the teahouse time stops—no past, no future. There is only now, and the letter is long overdue.

Dear Nakata-san:
Thank you for the wonderful baby albums you made
for Shinji. We were so happy to receive them when we
came to the orphanage. When I saw them, I realized
again how well he was looked after and cared for by
you at the orphanage. I was so grateful to you!

Shinji is such a happy boy. I am convinced that the
main reason he is so happy is that when he was younger
you took care of him and gave him so much love and
warmth. At that stage in his life, such a gift was a miracle.
I think he felt all your love and felt secure and safe. I don't
know how to thank you enough. I think you are really an
angel on earth.

If you want, we would like you to feel free to come
visit with Shinji any time you wish, and to continue to
have a close relationship with Shinji and to be in his life.
I know that right now he is bonding with us and that is
important, but you have been such an important part
of his life, too, and you are so welcome to develop the
relationship as he gets older, if you wish.

We know you are busy, but if you have some free
time, please come to spend any time with Shinji if you
wish. Or you can take him somewhere if you want. We
know he would love it.

I fold up the paper and walk it to the post office. I hope she
won't mind me reaching out.

Whose Tummy?

One winter night, Shinji and I are sitting on the couch, with Aska, getting ready for his bedtime story.

Tonight it's the tale of Momotaro, the Peach Boy, a Japanese classic. I've waited to share it because it's close to home.

As the wind blows outside, the branch of the cherry blossom scrapes lightly against the window. I think of Shogo's mother, reading him bedtime stories in this very same place, almost fifty years ago. Shinji snuggles into my arms.

"One day, an old woman goes outside to wash clothes in the river. Suddenly, a big peach floats downstream toward her. She picks it up and wraps it in her apron so she can carry it home to her husband. It's a big, beautiful peach, soft and ripe."

"I know this story," Shinji says. "I know what happens next."

I wonder if he's learned the story at the orphanage, or at kindergarten.

"What happens?" I ask.

"You say it," he replies.

I take a breath and continue.

"'What a perfect peach,'" the old man says.

But just as he's about to bite into it, a little boy leaps from the fruit onto the floor. The couple, who had long hoped for a child, raise the boy as their own. Many years pass. The boy grows big and strong. And when it's time for him to leave home to fight some demons, they say gokigenyo—farewell—without tears or regret."

"So then what?" Shinji asks.

I look at him, wonder if he's forgotten. But then again, there are many endings to the story, many ways to tell it.

"Eventually, the boy comes back, triumphant. The three live happily ever after," I say.

I close the book and turn to Shinji.

"What do you think? Did you like it?"

He turns to Aska, strokes her ears.

"It was all right," he says.

"But?"

"Well, you said I didn't come from your tummy, right?" he asks.

I take a breath. Not what I expected.

"That's right," I reply.

"Well," he says, "whose tummy did I come from?"

His question takes me by surprise, and I'm not sure how to answer.

I decide to tell the truth.

"Your birth mother's," I reply.

"I want to meet her," he says, biting his nails.

"I know. And hopefully, you will. Later."

"How much later?" he asks.

"Ummm," I say.

"When I'm as tall as you?"

"Taller. . . ."

We sit silently for a moment.

"If you meet her, what will you say to her?" I ask.

He bites his lip. "I'd thank her. I'd thank her for giving birth to me," he says.

"Really? Are you just saying that because you think that's what I want to hear?"

"No. Well, maybe," he says, smiling impishly.

I tuck him into bed, say goodnight, glad that we've talked about his birth mother. I want him to feel that he can ask questions, even if I might not have the answers.

The next day, a response from Nakata-san:

Dear Leza-san:
Thank you for your letter. I want to come to your
house and visit with you. I will be getting married and
moving to the countryside soon. Shinji was the first
child I had taken care of at the orphanage—that is why
it was hard for me to say goodbye. He will always be
with me.
                    S. *Nakata*

I put the letter in a scrapbook for Shinji so that some day he will
know his own story.

Sayonara

My father, stepmother, and half-sister come to visit. It's been over
a decade since Kyoko died and since my father last came. The old
house has been torn down, a new one built. Shogo's youngest sister
Hitomi, now thirty-seven, has moved out. She says she's happy to
finally fulfill her dream of starting her own aesthetic salon, happy
to be living on her own for the first time in her life. I'm suspicious
about this, know in part she's done it to make the space for Shinji,
to give him his own room. But I'm grateful nonetheless, and I'm
glad she's going to have the chance to fly.

Now my own half-sister Barbara is coming to Japan for the
first time. She's graduated from college and the trip is her gradu-
ation gift.

My father says our house feels like Northern California—with
its garden and decks. We've furnished it with wooden *tansu* and
crockery rescued from the torn-down houses in the neighborhood.
Only a foreigner would shamelessly retrieve things from the trash,

but I can't stand the thought of such treasures being crushed and hauled off to the dump.

Shinji takes them around the neighborhood, introduces them to the tofu seller, the dry cleaner, the vegetable man. Shogo cooks on the pots my father gave us for a wedding gift.

I become a tourist—viewing the city from a double-decker bus, going to the rotary sushi where you can pull what you want from a conveyer belt without having to speak any Japanese. I'm surprised to see California Rolls circle by. Ten years ago, they'd have been unheard of at a chain like this.

Over dinner one night, when we're all relaxed, I invite them to the yoga studio.

"I have no need to go there," my father says.

What does that mean? Is it because of his bad back? Why come five thousand miles and not go another five? Maybe he thinks that because he's been to our house, he doesn't have to go to the studio. I have no idea.

"I want you to. Please come for me," I say.

He shakes his head. "Can't do it," he says. And that is that.

I want to throttle him, to shake him, to help him. But I can't. I can't go there, can't repeat the conversation I've had with the family so many times over so many years. I've only ever been talking to myself.

Call me a slow learner, but I finally get it.

I don't have to try so hard anymore, to win his approval, or his love, or whatever.

I don't have to try at all. That's what Dietmar was talking about.

I let it go.

And then, later that night, I flip it.

I try to see what this could reflect in my own life. How many times had I come to the end of something and turned away before the finish line? How often had I given up because it was just too hard to take that final step? How many times had I not considered the other person, been unable to do something just for someone else? Because it was important or meaningful to them. So many times I couldn't count.

The following day, my stepmother and half-sister come to the yoga studio. They like the moon-window, the international mix of students. They say it's one of the highlights of their trip.

A few days later, it's time for them to leave.

Shogo, Shinji and I take them to the train station.

My father hugs me. "I'm proud of you," he says, tears in his eyes.

"You've taught me a lot," I say. It's not just a platitude. He's taught me that words and actions, no matter how small, are powerful and to be respected.

After seeing them off, Shogo and I walk back to our house, swinging Shinji between us.

"Where does the daytime go when it becomes night?" Shinji asks.

Shogo's explanation is scientific. "We have day and night because the Earth rotates. It takes twenty-four hours to turn. When the earth faces the sun, it's day. When it faces away from the sun, it's night."

Shinji nods.

"Day and night are paired together, like the sun and the moon," I say. Like dark and light, like fullness and emptiness.

I shiver in the cold. Shinji takes off his jacket, tries to make me wear it. But I refuse, as I don't want him to catch a cold. He insists, so I drape the little jacket over my shoulders.

We stop at the market to buy persimmons and pumpkins.

Shogo and I carry the shopping bags, which are overflow-ing with the beautiful orange fruits of fall. Shinji insists on taking all five of them, and won't move until we let him. He's weighed down like a pack mule; bags hanging off both arms. He wants to be strong. Stronger than strong. On some level, he knows how vulnerable he is, how vulnerable I am. He knows that I'm sad.

He reaches out to hold my hand.

It's the first time he's done this just for me. Not because he's scared, or upset. But because I am.

My heart aches with love for this little boy. *All of our happi-ness comes from thinking of others, and all our suffering comes from thinking only of ourselves.* I thank my meditation teacher for drill-ing this ancient wisdom from Master Shantideva into my brain. It is something Shinji seems to know. Something I need to be reminded of, over and over again.

Soon Shinji will be six, and he will have been our son for four years.

It's hard to remember the feeling of longing for him to arrive. It feels like he's always been with us.

Tiger Mom

The Year of the Tiger arrives. My year. I take Shinji to Tokyo Tower, the first time for both of us. It's Tokyo's knock-off of the Eiffel Tower, five hundred feet over the city. How small and insignificant I feel all the way up there, and how small even the hugest mega-complexes look below. The tower has a transparent glass floor that allows you to look straight down to the ground far below, but I'm not having any of it.

Shinji is fearless, tries to drag me onto it. I suggest instead that we go back down and jump on a trampoline on the first floor, where there's an entertainment center. Then I take him to a dumpy ramen stand where he has to sit on a stool to eat at the dirty counter. He's so tired he closes his eyes, falls backward off the stool and lands on the ground with a crash.

Thank God he has a thick skull and a great sense of humor.

We both laugh hysterically.

The next day is Rosh Hashana, so we go to Chabad House, where an Orthodox Jewish Rabbi from Israel and his wife, a Brooklyn-raised Rebbetzin, open their doors on Shabbat. They have six children, five of whom are boys. Shinji loves the atmosphere. Maybe it reminds him of the liveliness of the orphanage, the sharing, the games, the shenanigans. I watch Shinji play with the children, speaking a mixture of Japanese, English, and Hebrew. I love the Rebbetzin, who is an embodiment of calm wisdom, and who is very much her own person even in a situation where it would be easy and acceptable not to be.

Though I never thought I would attend Jewish services in Tokyo, especially at an Orthodox *shul*, this Rabbi is outgoing, open-minded, and positive, and his wife's strength, patience, and wisdom inspire me. They don't try to convert or judge. They accept me in my Indian dresses, shawl thrown over to cover up my arms. They welcome Shogo and Shinji, as they welcome everyone unconditionally. You come as you are. I go more often than I would have imagined.

Japanese men in *yarmulkes* sit at the table, breaking bread with the community of expats, Japanese, and Israelis. Together, we share a kosher meal of soup, Middle Eastern spreads, and homemade *challah*, warm from the oven. The Rabbi shares insights into the week's Torah portion, which happens to be the Akedah, in which God tests Abraham, who must bring his son Isaac to the altar for sacrifice.

This touches a nerve in me: Why would God need to test us, when he should know what's in our hearts already?

I ask the Rebbetzin about this. She says a test demands we go beyond what we believe is possible to endure. We can only pass such tests with faith and perseverance.

In the Torah, she explains, such tests prompt miracles. The Rebbetzin says that a miracle is what happens when God breaks out of a standard pattern of natural law and demonstrates unlimited power. A test is when God invites us to do the same.

People who pass tests cause miracles to happen, as God is empowering them to succeed. In the Torah, I discover that all great tests break barriers between creation and creator.

This makes sense to me: the idea that we can create our own lives, our own miracles. Even when struck by disaster, we can somehow find something redeeming and holy in the tragedy, the life that ensues.

Tests have been passed. There will be more in the future. I try to feel the sacredness of just listening to the Rabbi's prayers, the children's laughter. Just breathing. Being. In this moment is the possibility that the holy is in everything, no matter how difficult.

One cannot have faith without doubt, the Rebbetzin reminds me. One must arrive at faith through trust. One must travel into and through the doubt.

I wonder what Shinji will remember. What will define his "family story?" Will it all make sense to him someday?

I want to stack the deck in his favor.

I want to bring in more moments of light and joy.

March 11, 2011

Such thoughts are more or less abstractions until March 11, 2011. That's when the earth starts to shake and doesn't stop. I'm on the second floor of a five-story concrete building, eating lunch at a favorite café. As the temblor continues, I look around to see if anyone else is alarmed. No one is.

Tokyoites are famous for their calm in these situations, which are frequent and expected here. But the shaking continues and becomes more ferocious. I look at the woman at the table next to me. "I think we should get out!" I say. She nods and gathers her things. Together we flee down the stairs, two at a time.

As we run out onto the street, we're joined by people dashing from neighboring buildings. *This is it*, I think. I really do think my time is up.

The street buckles under us, and the four lanes of cars heading toward us slam on their brakes, each car rocking back and forth. It's surreal. The quake continues for two entire minutes. That's a long time for the earth to shake under your feet and the giant buildings around you to creak, rattle, and groan.

I think of Shinji in kindergarten, pray that he is safe. The building is strong, I hope. And Shogo, I hope he is okay. *I've got to get to Shinji!*

Two high-rises in the distance sway back and forth. I pray they don't fall, and that glass, concrete, metal, and debris don't rain down on the street. People take out their cell phones and punch in numbers helplessly, as the transmitters are down. I think of using my cell phone to take a video of the skyscraper swaying back and forth, but I can't take my eyes off it.

A woman next to me starts crying and screaming. I reach out to hug her. Comforting her somehow gives me comfort. I take deep breaths and try to stay centered. If I ever needed my yoga practice, it is now. Focusing on my breath reminds me that I'm still alive. As long as I have my breath, I'm safe. That's all I do, just try to stay calm and focused on my breath as I hold this stranger and calm her down.

When the shaking subsides, I run quickly to the yoga studio, which is just a block away. A Restorative class is in session, the students are still lying down over bolsters. The teacher hasn't evacuated; in Japan, they're taught to stay inside. I urge them to clear out. As one woman laces up her Converse high tops, a second big quake hits. The building supervisor is calmly going from door-to-door, making sure everyone is safe, without a concern for his own safety—even as the building starts to lurch and jolt. In the middle of the road is an open space normally reserved for waiting taxis. There are no taxis in sight, just a crowd of people sitting, standing, squatting, crying, and trying to use their cell phones. Of course, no one can.

Atershocks keep coming, and no one knows when another big one will hit.

I've got to go get Shinji! Now!

Normally it would be a ten-minute train ride to his school, but the trains have stopped running. By foot it will take me over an hour. I go as fast as I can, alternately running, sprinting, and walking to pace myself.

By the time I get to the school, the teachers tell me that my father-in-law has picked him up. Somehow, Shogo has been able to reach his father on a landline and ask him to get Shinji, even though the school is about a mile and a half from our house and my father-in-law is eighty. I'm so grateful that Ojiichan has come to pick up Shinji and that the teachers waited. I learn that some of the kids were very scared, and that the older kids like Shinji comforted the youngest. The teachers all have families of their own, but they stay until at 9 p.m., when the last child is picked up.

Once home, I try to remain calm, but there is no word from Shogo. The aftershocks are coming fast and furious, along with news of the devastation in the north from the tsunami. I don't want Shinji to panic, so we play cards and read stories and eat dinner with Ojiichan and open a Linzer torte from my friend Edgar, who now lives in Vienna, which I'd been saving for a "special occasion." Edgar's the one who encouraged me to call Shogo after I had canceled our first date. As the buttery, flaky crust melts in my mouth and mixes with the sweet unusual taste of elderberries, I think it just might be the best thing I've ever eaten.

We're lucky to still have gas and electricity. Many places don't. We even have Internet and can use the land line. I go on Facebook and offer our home to anyone stranded in the city, unable to get home. Others do the same. Later that night, Shogo comes home from work at the publishing company. It's taken him five hours on foot, but he's fine.

Everywhere I look, I see compassion in action. The usually bustling city of Tokyo is quiet and peaceful. There is no panic or looting. Rather, people are helping others and offering food, shelter, and supplies to those in need. A few days later, the staff at the convenience store apologizes for running out of supplies after people loaded up upon hearing of the damage to the nuclear plants and possible radiation.

In the coming days, friends abroad call and email, graciously offer us their homes. Many foreigners and some Japanese flee because of the uncertainty of the nuclear disaster and the continued quakes. France charters a plane for its citizens to leave. Our neighbors get on it. The U.S. Embassy issues a travel warning to those going to Japan. The Japanese government plans blackouts, but many are canceled because people conserve enough energy by turning off lights, turning the water off when they shower, reusing bath water, and so on, so that such blackouts are unnecessary. We realize we don't need to use half of the energy that we normally consume—and we don't use much. Others come to the same realization.

My mother calls, worried. I tell her we're fine. For now.

My father calls, urges us to leave. Says he wants us to be safe. He says he loves me, says he always has.

I'm about to hang up the phone, when I remember what my teacher said: *If we want to see a world without war and violence, we have to quell the anger in our own hearts first.*

I say, "I love you, too."

Aftershocks

For the next few weeks. Tokyo continues to shake. Thousands of aftershocks, some as big as 7.2, rattle Japan. The stark reality of the four nuclear meltdowns comes to light.

Shogo and I talk about what to do.

He says he wants to stay. We should remain calm and not panic. He feels he has a responsibility to his father, his family. The old eldest son—*chonan*—story, again. There's no question that he will stay and deal with whatever arises, samurai-style. Though he worries about radiation, he also seems to meet the possible dangers with a sense of acceptance and stoicism. He's fifty-two.

Then he says, "But if you want to leave and take Shinji, you should."

Again, the ball is in my court.

I weigh the options—split up my family, or stay with Shogo and ride it out.

Is it safe for children to be here? Unsafe? Am I putting my beloved child in danger?

Will this be a decision I will regret? After all we've gone through to have a family, is it worth it?

We comb the news reports, sift through the misinformation, the hype, the doomsday reports from abroad, the sobering facts from experts in the field, the lies from the government and electric company.

With the earth still shaking, and the nuclear reactors far from stable, the situation is dangerous, there's no denying that. More foreigners leave. I don't fault them for it at all.

I look around me. How are my Japanese neighbors reacting? Most are stoic, resigned. They help each other. They band together. The mothers are out with their children, in the parks, at the schools, carrying on. Are they incredibly brave, or seriously in denial?

I feel the weight of my freedom. I have a choice to leave. Most of them probably don't.

I take a wait-and-see approach. I tell Shogo that if I feel at any point we are putting Shinji's life in danger, I will be on the first plane out of here. He agrees.

Shogo feels that if we're going to stay here, we might as well be useful. I keep the yoga studio open to offer a place for my students. Em teaches bravely. I am scared to go back into the building, but inspired by her and the students.

I go in to teach. As we lift our arms overhead and move into Sun Salutations, the walls start to shake violently, the building creaks as it shudders. We stop and breathe, wondering: *Is this my last breath? Is it over?*

"Aren't you scared?" I ask my students.

"No. We are here now. Even if we leave our bodies, this is our fate," a few of them say.

I'm completely blown away by their attitude. And I've been calling myself their teacher?

I pray that the shaking and leaking will stop.

Home

Nakata-san calls to check on Shinji.

She and her boyfriend have married and have moved back to the countryside. The orphanage will soon be a distant memory for them, too.

Other marriages break up after the quake—people who have been "enduring" realize that life is too short to suffer. Conversely, some couples on the fence get married. As time goes by and concerns of radiation mount, more people leave. I wonder what to do.

I'd moved to Japan in part because it was safe. Now that it is clearly unsafe, can I still consider it home?

But what of California? There are certainly quakes, and fault lines abound. And crime as well—more than in Japan.

But really, are we ever safe? A main practice of Tibetan Buddhism is death meditation. The point is to rid ourselves of false security and embrace the moment. The saying is: *The fact of our death is certain. We just don't know the time or the place.*

I lie on the ground and go into this practice. I see myself dead. I picture the people I love around me, hear their words about my life.

What have I done for others? What have I done that is lasting, beyond myself?

We visualize our death to rid ourselves of delusions of immortality. To become aware, on a visceral level, that our body is impermanent, that death could come at any moment. When we feel this in meditation, we come into direct contact with our fears, our numbness, our laziness, our excuses, our blockages to living more fully.

Seeing ourselves dead, we realize that, in fact, we don't have much time left. We'd better live every moment, let go of that which needs to fall away so we can become more alive.

The only chance for survival is to face our fears and grow larger than them. Embrace them, as a mother would hug a difficult child.

Shogo is my life. Shinji is my life.

They belong here, and I belong here with them.

I'm staying.

The Rabbi's wife reminds me of the Talmudic adage that we each go through life with two notes in our pockets. One says, "For me the world was created." The other says, "I am but dust."

Our work is to live in the balance, and when the world tips us too much in either direction, to try to right ourselves.

Why the Caged Bird Sings

One morning over breakfast of brown rice and miso soup, I ask Shinji if I can write something down on a piece of origami paper lying on the table.

He says I can. I do, then go back to eating.

"What did you write?" he asks.

I tell him I wrote down "I Know Why the Caged Bird Sings." It's the title of Maya Angelou's first novel. I think of it because I'm writing this book, and I remember when she came to my elementary school more than forty years ago.

"Why does the caged bird sing?" Shinji asks, waving his hand in front of my face, bringing me back to the present.

"It wants to be free," I reply.

"Yeah, that's true," he says, mulling it over.

"But . . . ?" I sense a "but." "What do you think?"

"Well, I think four things," he says, twisting his lip.

"Tell me," I say. "I'm listening."

"One," he counts on his fingers. "It cries for family. Two: to say 'it's my territory'—it wants to protect its 'nest.' Three: it's a bird, so birds sing, even in cages. Four: it sings for itself."

I nod, taking in his words. The caged bird sings to stay alive, to hope. But I like Shinji's understanding. Where did this knowledge come from? He loves to watch TV nature shows, but I don't think that's where he got this. Somehow, he already has a wisdom that has taken me fifty years to learn. He has it somewhere deep in his own heart, in a place that's neither Berkeley nor Tokyo—a place where the impossible is possible, a place where anything can happen.

It's a place I want to go, and stay forever.

I re-read Angelou's novel. I want to take myself back to that time in my own life and make peace with it so I can keep moving forward.

Back then, in 1970, before she'd read her poetry at Clinton's inaguration, before she'd become a national treasure, she'd come to our school to speak of how the power of her words had frightened her—she'd believed they had the power to take life.

Well, they did. But they also had the power to give life.

What power that woman's words had on this little awestruck girl sitting on the floor at Malcolm X auditorium, at a time when I hated being me.

Her visit gave me hope.

She modeled how to turn the straw of your life into gold. She showed us how to lift others up when you flew. She had every reason to be angry, self-righteous. But she wasn't. When asked why she never became embittered, she said she'd "always felt loved."

I don't even remember what she said that day. I just remember the way her voice reverberated against the walls of my heart. In that moment, I fell in love with her, and I think I fell in love with poetry. I felt the ferocious, undeniable power of words.

"I've learned that people will forget what you said, people will forget what you did, but people will never forget how you made them feel," she famously said. I know this is true, because when Maya came to my elementary school and spoke, she was doing just that—Speaking Directly To Me. Speaking to that small voice in myself that others would later try to silence, that voice which I would use for years to silence myself. That voice in Maya which had grown until it became so powerful and life-affirming that it could only be let out to sing. And sing it did. For everyone.

And even though it took me many years to free my own heart, on that day a seed had been planted.

Letting Go

Spring comes, and the cherry blossoms confetti to the ground. I take Shinji back to Tokyo Tower. This time, Shogo comes, too.

"Let's go," I say, inching out onto the transparent platform.

"I'll hold your hand," Shinji promises, stepping in front of me to lead the way.

"Okay," I say. Then I step out, heart pounding. The ground is five hundred feet below us, the buildings small as toy houses.

Shinji reaches back for my hand. I take it.

Shogo's, too.

I plant my feet on the ground, rooting them in the earth. I look down at this magnificent world, this mandala we've somehow created together, and I feel happy and safe.

I have everything I thought I wanted, and more.

I have a strong, solid marriage. I have a career. I've seen the world. I've healed my relationship with my family. And last but not least, I've found myself in the least likely of places—Japan.

And because I feel safe, I can walk out into the unknown.

I let go of Shinji and Shogo's hands.

I know they're with me, by my side.

I know I'm finally free to embrace the *ma*, the mother within.

I open my arms wide, offering up all that I am.

REFERENCES

Ayukawa, Nobuo. *America and Other Poems: Selected Poetry by Ayukawa Nobuo*. Translated by Leza Lowitz and Shogo Oketani. Los Angeles: Kaya Press, 2007.

Brandeis, Gayle. *Fruitflesh: Seeds of Inspiration for Women Who Write*. San Francisco: Harper San Francisco, 2002.

Desikachar, Kausthub. *The Yoga of the Yogi*. Chennai, India: Krishnamacharya Yoga Mandiram, 2005.

Forrest, Ana T. *Fierce Medicine*. New York: HarperCollins, 2011.

Gyatso, Geshe Kelsan. *Meaningful to Behold: View, Meditation and Action in Mahayana Buddhism: An Oral Commentary to Shantideva's "A Guide to the Bodhisattva's Way of Life (Bodhisattvacharyavatara)."* Ulverston, Cumbria: Wisdom Publications, 1980.

Judith, Anodea. *Eastern Body, Western Mind: Psychology and the Chakra System as a Path to the Self*. Berkeley: Celestial Arts, 2004.

Kapnek Rosenberg, Shelley. *Adoption and the Jewish Family: Contemporary Perspectives*. Philadelphia: The Jewish Publication Society, 1998.

Kawainui Kane, Herb. *Pele: Goddess of Hawaii Volcanoes*. Captain Cook, HI: Kawainui Press, 1987.

Lafferty, Kimberley Theresa. "Learning to Fly." Lecture at Yoga Kula, Brooklyn, NY, October 22, 2012.

Lamott, Anne. *Grace (Eventually): Thoughts on Faith*. New York: Penguin, 2007.

Lipman, Kennard, Ph.D. *Kingdoms of Experience: The Four Worlds of Kabbalah as Prayer and Meditation*. Berkeley: Arts and Letters Press, 2011.

Lowitz, Leza. *Yoga Poems: Lines to Unfold By*. Berkeley: Stone Bridge Press, 2000.

———and Reema Datta. *Sacred Sanskrit Words: For Yoga, Chant and Meditation*. Berkeley: Stone Bridge Press, 2004.

Mogel, Wendy. *The Blessing of a Skinned Knee: Using Jewish Teachings to Raise Self-Reliant Children*. New York: Scribner, 2008.

Mutkananda, Swami. Sivananda Ashram Lecture. Rishikesh, India, 2007.

Osho. *The Book of Woman*. London: Penguin, 2002.

Shapiro, Dani. *Devotion: A Memoir*. New York: HarperCollins, 2010.

Simpson, Liz. *The Book of Chakra Healing*. New York: Sterling, 1999.

Srivatsa, Ramaswami, and David Hurwitz. *Yoga Beneath the Surface: An American Student and His Indian Teacher Discuss Yoga Philosophy and Practice*. New York: Marlowe and Company, 2006.

Tate-Stratton, Danielle. "Adopting a Child from Japan." Being a Broad Newsletter (Tokyo), no. 26 (November 2007).

Trungpa, Chogyam Rinpoche. *Smile at Fear*. Boston: Shambhala, 2010.

Zalman, Shneur, Rabbi of Liadi. *Machzor for Rosh Hashana*. Brooklyn: Lubavitch Chassidic Prayerbooks Corporation, 2006.

ACKNOWLEDGMENTS

This book is a work of memory, an individual process. Two people who experienced the same event will remember it—and tell
it—differently. The events described herein are how I remember
and experienced them, although the timeline has sometimes been
altered for readability, and certain people's names/identities have
been changed for the sake of privacy.

I wrote this book to record how my family came to be so that
one day my son could know me better, and so that I would not
forget. I also wanted to offer this story in the hope that it might
help anyone struggling in a similar way. In the end, this is just one
adoptive mother's quest. There are hundreds of such stories all
over the world, like the one I received from my friend Dick Allen
of Petaluma:

> *Dear Leza:*
> *You might appreciate this thing I wrote a month or so*
> *ago on the way back from Guatemala.*
>
> *If you like love stories, you must love airports. Just get*
> *there early and look around you.*
>
> *She, obviously American, is in line, a very slow line,*
> *at the Guatemala City airport, with her husband. They're*
> *also leaving. They are forty or so—a thin line of hair along*
> *her part shows some gray. From the glow on her face and*

the way her arms envelop the small baby girl with radiant black eyes and hair that reflects the morning light, she's holding something unimaginably precious. It's as if she's caught the golden ring, finally, after so many cycles on the carousel. The child, five or six months old, looks out at the world, her eyes curious, sparkling. She already confidently smiles back at the stranger admiring her. She is safe and knows she is loved.

It is a scene so beautiful, so radiant. My heart fills, as do my eyes now remembering how it is to hold one's very own new child.

No Renaissance painter with all his skill, not Leonardo, Michelangelo, or Raphael at their very best, ever captured this love of Madonna and child, even after adding golden halos.

I wonder: do moms at home, who easily conceive and receive their babies as predictably and easily as high school diplomas, also feel such fulfillment, such gratefulness?

Three hours later, walking the aisle somewhere over the Atlantic, I see them again, huddled together as one at the back of the plane. Do I tell her what I have written? Would it be intrusive? I decide to take the risk. I go back to my seat and copy over the above, as clearly as I can. Then I go and present what I hope will be received as a gift to her, to them. She quietly and slowly reads, then turns to me with tears in her eyes and says, "Thank you. We're keeping a scrapbook for her and this will be part of it."

You never know where grace will appear.

* * *

Grace has appeared in so many ways along this journey—so many people guided and supported me. Special thanks first and foremost to my partner Shogo, whose love never wavers. Gratitude to the late Donald Richie, my family, my sisters, and to yoga teachers Veera Wibaux, Jill Edwards Minyé, Eric Brinkman, Gaye Abbott, Simone Simon, Kimberley Theresa, and Ted Lafferty, and to all the great teachers and healers who helped me find my way.

Em Bettinger—thank you for somehow typing up a manuscript from notes scribbled on napkins and the backs of subway tickets. Thank you to Liane Wakabayashi for countless hours of painstaking editing, for reminding me of the laws of *lashon hora*, and for holding me to a higher standard of positive speech. Deni Béchard, Maud Winchester, Colleen Sakurai, Judith Fairchild, Christopher Yohmei Blasdel, Ted Taylor, Clara Chare, Abigail Davidson, Richard Ruben, Stephanie Culen, Marie Doezema, Helen Tashman, Jacinta Hin, Catherine Harper-Tee, Joan Taschian, Tracy Slater, Toshiko Yanagihara, Tomoko Kawahara, Phil Barnett, Doug Powers, Manfred, A. Polk, E. Feldman, Sharon Mann, Cathy Layne, Amanda Giacomini, Eisa Davis, Angelica Kushi, Haruka Takahashi, Sachiyo Munechika, Kiyoko Ogawa, Windi Braden, Fred Schodt, Nina Zolotow, Ralph and Daissy Koch, Sara Shivani, Eko Smith, Motoyuki Shibata, Phil Bettinger, Wadada Leo Smith, Sunyoung Lee, Ruth Ingulsrud (crackerjack proofreader!), and Donna and David Mendelsohn offered invaluable support or feedback on drafts of this manuscript over the years.

The staff and students at Sun and Moon Yoga have been my sanity, while Rabbi and Rebbetzin Edery offered a warm community in Tokyo to explore my Jewish roots. (Thanks again to Liane for bringing me back into the fold.) Congregation Beth Shalom of Napa Valley also graciously welcomed us as family.

Kelly Falconer of Asia Literary Agency and Peter Goodman of Stone Bridge Press have been my Dream Agent and Publisher. The staff of Stone Bridge Press—Linda Ronan, Michael Palmer, Robert Koeze—made the rest of the work of publishing (after writing) all the more rewarding and enjoyable. Thank you!

Pranams to my BHS peeps, and to the Amma posse—Shiva Rea, Daphne, Coral, Kelley, and Debra. Gratitude to River of Sound leader Gina Salá, and bunkmates Lori, Leah, Annette, Jens, and Soren. Thanks to editors Suzanne Kamata and Nancy Cleary, who published a portion of this book in their anthology, *Call Me Okaasan: Adventures in Multicultural Mothering*; Kaitlin Quist-gaard, Jennifer Sweeney, and Philip Armour, who did the same in *Yoga Journal*; Melvin McLeod and Andrea Miller, who published early excerpts in *Shambhala Sun* and *Best Buddhist Writing*; Gina Misrogou and Huntington Sharp, who sent my work to *The Huffington Post;* Erica Lyons of *Asian Jewish Life*; Shannon Young and Signal 8 Press of *How Does One Dress to Buy Dragonfruit*; KJ Dell'Antonia of the *New York Times* "Motherlode" blog; Eugene Tarshis of *Wingspan*; Naoko Tajima, Hiromi Miyazawa, and Joy Yu Natsume of *Yoga Journal Japan*; and Jennifer Pastiloff of The Manifest-Station.

I'm grateful to Elizabeth Floyd for accompanying me to that dark, smoky jazz bar so many years ago and to Edgar Honetschläger for going to bat for Shogo. Deep appreciation to the staff and social workers at the orphanage and the CGC—miracle workers, all. And finally, I'm especially grateful to our son, without whom there would be no story.

L.L.

LEZA LOWITZ is an accidental global citizen—bicultural mother, modern yogini, and multi-genre author of over seventeen books. She has received the APALA Award in Young Adult Litera- ture, the Japan-U.S. Friendship Commission Prize for the Trans- lation of Japanese Literature, the PEN Oakland Josephine Miles Award for Poetry, a Translation Fellowship from the National Endowment for the Arts, a California Arts Council Individual Fellowship in Poetry, a National Endowment for the Humanities Independent Scholar Fellowship, and the PEN Syndicated Fiction Award. Among her popular books are *Yoga Poems: Lines to Unfold By* and *Jet Black and the Ninja Wind*. Her work has also appeared in *The New York Times*, *Yoga Journal*, *Yoga International*, *Sham- bhala Sun*, *The Best Buddhist Writing*, *The Huffington Post*, and *The Japan Times*. *Up from the Sea*, her Young Adult novel in verse about Japan's March 11, 2011, earthquake and tsunami, will be published by Crown Books for Young Readers/Penguin Random House in 2016.

Leza lives in Tokyo where she runs a yoga studio, tends her century-old garden, and cares for her young son, husband, and two half-wild wolf dogs.